HOURGLASS

THE MACMILLAN COMPANY
NEW YORK • BOSTON • CHICAGO
DALLAS • ATLANTA • SAN FRANCISCO

MACMILLAN AND CO., LIMITED
LONDON • BOMBAY • CALCUTTA
MADRAS • MELBOURNE

**THE MACMILLAN COMPANY
OF CANADA, LIMITED**
TORONTO

HOURGLASS
Stories of a Measured Year

BY

JOHN W. LYNCH

AUTHOR OF *A Woman Wrapped in Silence*
AND *This Little While*

THE MACMILLAN COMPANY
New York   1952

Acknowledgment for the use of quoted material is made by the author to the following publishers and authors:

To *The Catholic World* for "The Day Of The Chains," copyright 1934, for "Confessions At Seven-thirty," copyright 1934, and for "Prayer At Early Mass," copyright 1936, all copyrighted by *The Catholic World*.

To The Oxford University Press and the family of the poet for *The Poems of Gerard Manley Hopkins*, copyright 1948 by The Oxford University Press, Inc.

To Rinehart and Company, Inc. for lines from "Metropolitan Nightmare," in *Selected Works of Stephen Vincent Benét*, copyright 1933 by Stephen Vincent Benét.

To Charles Scribner's Sons for lines from *The Works of Francis Thompson*, copyright 1913 by Charles Scribner's Sons.

To *America* for "Humiles," and to the Vincentian Fathers of Philadelphia for "The Assumption."

To Saint Joseph

I am soft sift
In an hourglass . . . at the wall
Fast, but mined with a motion, a drift. . . .

The title and the seasonal headings are derived from the poetry of Gerard Manley Hopkins; and, while I am sure that Father Hopkins, had he known that his work would be put to such use, would wince, I am also certain that, such was his charity, he would have consented.

J. W. L.

CONTENTS

PART I

PART II

HOURGLASS

The times are nightfall, look their light grows less;
The times are winter, watch, a world undone:

TO LEARN IS HOLY: TO TEACH, DIVINE

THE immediate object of any man who sets himself down to write is to so order his words that he will be understood, and the ultimate ideal of any man who writes, so the stylists say, is to so compose his paragraphs that he cannot be misunderstood. This book admittedly often falls short of the immediate object; it will never, even with diligent use of the dictionary, come close to the ultimate ideal.

However, on this present subject there are several classes of people who, presuming they read these pages at all, will not only understand but will understand so intimately that they cannot mistake the force of the argument presently to be made.

The first of these would be the composers of advertising copy, if there be any among us today, or, lacking them, any and all who have listened to the commercials inserted in radio and TV programs. The advertiser has an idea to promote. Essentially it is a very simple thing: that Grumblies Are Cooked by Moonlight . . . They Make Your Breakfast Beam: that Whistler Cars Give Mother Atomic Transportation: that Wheew Is The Rinse For You: that Super-Shoes Are Super-News. Whatever the product or the content of the Message about it, the total job of explanation is not too complicated. And yet advertising is a highly paid profession. Conferences are held, plans and campaigns are formulated. The psychologists are consulted. And the boys must worry about how far they are heeded because they are at it so incessantly, which is why we have worked the radio listeners into this . . . they can testify that this simple attempt at a simple thing is belabored, repeated, dinned and hollered, crooned, rhymed and dittied as if the advertisers despaired of ever convincing, ever making the sales proposition stick. So first in our special audience, we greet the advertising people, both practitioners and victims.

The second group of our understanding readers would be the teachers, Heaven bless them. They know. They will get the point. The job of the teacher is to get History A, or Social Science C, or even what is known as Plane Geometry, through some twenty or thirty youthful heads. Is it easy? Do they succeed? Is the struggle, nay, the pitched battle, worth the money? Ask them when they are free to talk. Invite them to unveil their souls. You'll find out. Teaching is patient, enduring, bitter work, and when you have it all completed, you are not sure you have done anything. The resistance of the human mind to knowledge is a notable characteristic.

Then we would summon all folk who have ever been Chairmen for the Annual Chowder and Pickle Festival, and who have ever been in a position of explaining the Committee's plans to the assembled Club. The Chairman announces that they will all meet at the Corner of Main and Willow at 10 A.M.; the Junior Members Bringing Rolls Unbuttered, the Senior Members Bringing Hot Dogs, the Officers Bringing Pickles: and the poor man is understood by 42 per cent of the club to have said that the Junior Members will bring the Corner of Willow and Main, the Senior Members will roll unbuttered at 10 P.M., while the Officers will be pickled.

By all means the Chairman of the Clothing Drive, the Paper Drive, the Community Plan for Post-War Reconfusion, the Thanksgiving Basket Council, and the Card Club Outing are among our most appreciative readers on the subject we shall shortly broach.

But before we get into it, there is one more class of mankind who will surely be sensitive to the implications of our approaching discourse. They are the Pastors of Churches. They will understand for, at intervals, they announce the Hours for the Masses on the Holy Day, and then sit up half the night answering the phone to correct the impression they seem to have given that the seven o'clock Mass will be said at 7:38; the nine o'clock will be said either at 9:45 or entirely omitted; and that the noon Mass will be delayed till 12:07 because of two Albanian altar boys and the complication of advanced time. Yes, the Pastors will know, and although for dignity I am reluctant, I shall generously include the Assistants. They will know too, insofar as they are capable.

All of these people, therefore, whose special duty is to convey information to somebody, we expect will be our most sympathetic readers for while the general public may, in a measure, understand, advertisers, teachers, committees and pastors will give unanimous and ardent consent to our proposition. It is this: the success of the Catholic Church in teaching religion to the whole world amounts to a constant miracle so huge that it marks the Church as divine. The very knowledge of the Creed, the sheer recognition of Catholic morality, the mere knowledge of the Ten Commandments and the Seven Sacraments, possessed as it is possessed by millions of human minds, constitutes a more than human achievement.

If you want to be sure that the Church was founded by God, just consider how many people know about Christianity. I make no distinction as to the degree of the knowledge, for instance, as between a theologian and a child in the fourth grade, nor do we here reflect on the use of the knowledge towards sanctity and happiness. We point here merely to the fact that millions of people do know of the contents of Catholic teaching. That is something. When you look at it sharply, it is startling, almost a fifth identifying mark for the Church of Christ.

Religion is not a simple subject. Religion can't be summed up in an advertiser's slogan to be repeated over and over. Religion is much more complex than geometry or biology. It is more than an easy program for some action and somewhat broader than even the most involved parish regulations.

Merely to present the basic tenets of religion, just think of what the Church has had to do. First, there is the nature of God and the relationship of the world to Him. Then there must be information as to the nature of man, the purpose of life, the immorality of the soul, the significance of the human will. We have not even started yet, for religion must go on to tell of vice and virtue, the nature and purpose of Our Lord's visit to the world, the foundation of the Church, and the fact of Priesthood. The necessity of Grace, the sources of Grace in the Sacraments, and the great meaning of the Great Sacrament which is Christ in the Eucharist. Penance, Judgment. Heaven and Hell for final solution. The prayers, the very common prayers of the Our Father, the Hail Mary and the Creed. The chief incidents of the Gospel story. The Commandments of God. The Commandments of the Church. All these are a part of religion and we have not ended yet.

We ought to include the Mass in our summary, for it is a fact that millions attend every week. We should not omit the Friday abstinence, for that is observed by millions also, and both the Mass and Friday involve Calvary and the Redemption. By the way, we have not mentioned the Redemption yet nor the Fall of humanity in its first critical trial. Indeed, religion is complex, many sided, in its very content and even when we leave out all the reasoning and history and the philosophy which support it.

This is what the Church has actually taught to millions and millions of minds, of all nationalities, of all capabilities and ages! It's a gigantic and complicated task, and while the propagation of the Faith is a continuing process, while we fret our consciences in seeking means and methods to improve in effectiveness, we can, for this once, pause to observe what the Church has actually done. It is an even bigger job than we realize, for the knowledge of

Christianity outside of the Catholic Church is an effect of the Church.

The Church carried the Faith through the centuries and delivered its content everywhere to the present. When a man blasphemes in the Holy Name, he is giving unconscious tribute to the Church that made the Holy Name known. When a movie audience universally recognizes what an actor is doing when he makes the Sign of the Cross, when a Roman collar identifies a man on a bus, when rosary beads are descriptive to a nurse in an emergency ward, the Church is receiving a compliment for the fact that it has taught the world a doctrine.

Perhaps this is the least of tributes which the Church has earned. Certainly we are forever engaged in the effort at accuracy and in teaching away persistent error about the Faith, but it is still true that the actual dissemination of knowledge, the informational job, if you will, is of magnificent proportions. Ask any teacher, ask any advertising agency, and ask any poor, harried soul who sweats it out at a railroad information desk. They will tell you.

THE CROSS AND THE CRIB

One of the good things about a cold, blustery day is that, hurrying for home at supper time, you are grateful, having made it, for warmth and lights and the smell of cooking. On this particular day, in addition to the steaming pans on the back of the stove, the housekeeper had been busy about the Christmas pine and the evergreens. The little figures of the saints on the mantelpiece were banked with branches, with a poinsettia valiant in the midst. It is surprising how much of Christmas in these northern climes is in the care for proper decoration. The season begins when the first wreath is hung. This instinct of preparation, of course, is very Catholic and leads eventually, and in climax, to gold vestments and laces and boughs swung in a sanctuary for a Midnight Mass. We need not, at the moment, go far into that, but only say that by some chance a wooden crucifix on the wall also was made ready for Christmas. That had been decorated too.

A single branch of pine, convex in shape and large enough to spread above and below, had been fastened as a background for the cross. Three or four red berries hung on the green needles and altogether it looked like heraldry, as if the branch were a shield with the cross emblazoned on it to make an emblem. The arrangement recalled pictures of one of those wayside shrines in Bavaria or the Tyrol where the crucifix is covered by a narrow, slanting roof and snow has fallen. There was no peaked roof over this crucifix and we did not have snow in the room, even for Christmas, but there was a sense of innocence, a sense of the Faith about the combination of the branch and the berries and the cross that suggested a shrine in a land where the Church is old and beloved as a daily presence.

When you think of it, this is the Crucifixion seen against the distant background of Bethlehem. As if, on that fateful Friday, a wreath had been hung on the crossbar; as if carols were sung against the thunder; and as though angels had come again and choired of peace and men of good will over Calvary. The crucifix is a stark symbol, and you think of sins and failure and the summons to penance when you see it, but with the Christmas pine behind it, somehow it was softened and lightened.

The Crucifixion against the vision of Bethlehem! As if among the soldiers, shepherds had returned. As if an ox had wandered up that hill. As if Joseph were here, and as if Mary, full of grace, had kept with her a lullaby from the night of the Star and had brought it here with her in the pain; as if the sharp joy and the ecstasy and the wonder of the Crib had been preserved, and she held them now in her grief, like a light, like a center of light shining here in the great darkness. As if part of the strength that let her be at the Cross was the memory of the bliss of His infant face; as if His Birth supported her for His Death.

We do not know, and certainly we must not strain the sense of the Scripture, but it is written of her that *"she kept all these things, pondering them in her heart,"* and might we not think that she never forgot the Midnight even at that dense and overwhelming midnight of mid-afternoon? That she could endure His scars for memory of *"the swaddling clothes"*? He spoke to her on Calvary, and the word He said to John is the word we claim and hold with John, but which He gave to her as her own. *"Son, behold thy mother."* That in His word, Bethlehem was implicit, summoned now, and offered for a comfort? That she remembered gold and frankincense and myrrh when He had come to His last and utter poverty?

But the Christmas branch behind the cross does tell one thing certainly which Mary knew and which the Church has been teaching ever since. Both of these moments, the silent night and the quaking April day were made by the strange and eternal love of God for mankind. The crib and the Incarnation were prelude to the cross; the Redemption and Calvary are conclusion for Bethlehem. The promise of the one spoken by the angels is fulfilled in the other when He said: *"It is finished."*

Long before, a prophet had linked them both in God's meaning: *"I know the thoughts that I think of thee; yea, I have loved thee with an everlasting love."*

SONG FOR SUNDAY MORNING

IN THE Saturday evening editions newspapers usually print a summary of the religious schedules for the following day. Beyond doubt the dullest reading in this section, and always the shortest, is the heading: Roman Catholic.

It reads like a railroad timetable. There is nothing but the name of the church, the address, and a list of the hours of the Masses. No sermon titles. No account of the speaker, or the guest speaker. No musical program. Nothing except that bare list of the hours.

And it is the same list for fifty-two Saturday evening editions a year.

Probably you have never paused to look at the Roman Catholic section on the Saturday night religious page, for this would have a news value only for a stranger in town, some passing guest in a hotel, somebody who needed to find out where and when he could get to Mass between trains. But try it next Saturday. Read the list all the way down. Get the rhythm of it, the swing, the lilt of it. The very monotony makes magnificent and significant sound. This is like the tolling of a bell, the repeating fall of an accent in music.

It goes like this: Cathedral: Masses, 7, 8, 9, 10, 11. Assumption: Masses, 5:45, 7, 8, 9, 10, 11. Blessed Sacrament: Masses, 7, 8, 9, 10, 11. That's the theme, the motif, the recurring basic phrase . . . 7, 8, 9, 10, 11. Then there is a quick change for the list reads: Holy Trinity: Masses, 8 and 9:30 before the rhythm gets into the variation, the syncopation of Most Holy Rosary: Masses, 6, 7:30, 8:30, 9:45, 11. Then the steady beat of the theme is discovered again in Our Lady of Pompeii: Masses, 7, 9, 10 and 11, omitting, you will note, the stroke of 8, when trippingly in quickstep, like a jig, comes St. James: Masses, 6:15, 7:30, 8:30 and 10:30. Then the steady rhythm returns with St. Anthony of Padua: Masses, 7, 8, 9, 10, 11.

You could keep it up and quote here the entire listing, but we don't want to spoil the fun. Read it for yourself. . . . The Song of Sunday Morning: 7, 8, 9, 10, 11. The Chant of the Living Church, 7, 8, 9, 10, 11. The Rhyme of the Ancient Faith, 7, 8, 9, 10, 11.

But having enjoyed the sheer music of that simple listing, then to get the full meaning of the song you have to let your imagination run on a little. This is the schedule that is known by heart . . . a beautiful expression, known by heart . . . in all the families of the parish. These are the schedules that cause such remarks as, "I'm going to the seven. You watch the baby, and then you can go to the nine." Or, "I'm going to receive in the morning and I'll set the clock for the eight." Or, "I'm tired tonight. I'll sleep till the eleven." Catholic language, the calm, easy speaking of the normal Faith. 7, 8, 9, 10, 11.

This is the crowd hurrying down the street, the search for a place to park, the joyful assembly and gathering of people who can never be strangers to each other. This is the brushing of hats and clothes, the pulling on of gloves, the hasty daub of powder and rouge, the closing of the front door, the putting of the envelope in the purse. This is Sunday morning up to noon in any city in the United States, in any weather.

There is so much in that weekly, nameless list. This is a city full of priests, fasting, assigned to an altar and an hour, going to sleep on the Saturday night, rising to keep the eternal tryst at an altar stone. This is lives dedicated to the continuation of the Sacrifice first offered at Calvary and at the table of the Last Supper. This is a pastor solicitous for the structure of a church, the long, common labor of planning that a church might stand at an address in the city, the multitude of contributions that maintain the buildings and keep them worthy of the worship of God. These are the traditions of a parish, the affections, the loyalties over the years. This is a family going by habit to a certain location in the building every Sunday, even now when pew rent is largely a method of the past.

This is the vision of the green of the vestments changing to the white, to the purple, to the red as the months proceed: the sound of the ringing of Mass bells through all the morning. This is the central silence and the hush in which the three-fold ringing comes, first for the lifted Host, then for the lifted Chalice.

Behind this brief, compact printing of a schedule each Saturday night, is the tremendous, two-thousand-year-old teaching. A whole world of doctrine is implicit here.

That God is: that God seeks His people: that God Who sought His people by being born a Man at Bethlehem offered Himself as a Gift to be worth more than the debt of His people's sins: that God gave Himself in Gift on the Cross at Calvary: that the Gift of Himself He made continuous under the aspect of Bread and beneath the appearance of Wine: that a priest is joined by people, and all are joined to Christ, as priest and people and Christ offer the Gift of Himself in worship at 7, 8, 9, 10, and 11 . . . fifty-two Sundays a year.

If you read this schedule next Saturday night, as we have suggested, you can hear some echoes that come after. Out from Sinai will come the sound of the First of the Ten Commandments: "*I am the Lord Thy God: thou shalt not have strange Gods before Me.*" Then the voice of Christ will speak in the words He uttered: "*on a very high mountain*" when He had been shown "*all the kingdoms of the world.*" . . . "*The Lord thy God shalt thou adore and Him only shalt thou serve.*" You can hear, too, in echo the nearer voice of Christ: "*And the Bread which I shall give is my Flesh for the life of the world.*" And: "*Do this for a commemoration of Me.*" And: "*Going therefore, teach ye all nations . . . and behold I am with you all days even unto the consummation of the world.*" And beyond the echo of the voice of Christ will begin the sounding of St. Paul: "*For as often as you shall eat this bread, and drink this chalice, you shall show the death of the Lord until He come. Therefore whosoever shall eat this bread, or drink of the chalice of the Lord unworthily, shall be guilty of the body and the blood of the Lord.*"

And after Paul will be the ancients of the Church, the Fathers of the Faith, before there was any America, or newspapers, or an English language. They will all sound in the same exhorting, on an identical insistence for this is the Faith now, as the Faith has been since the beginning. Seven, eight, nine, ten and eleven . . . *even unto the consummation of the world.*"

"JOY TO MY YOUTH"

CHRISTMAS is over now. The wreaths have come to that appearance of reminiscence common to them, and the poinsettias and the pine trees, along about December 29th and after. The wrappings are all discarded, the ribbons are bunched in a tangle and thrown away, the cards are beginning to gather dust and forgetfulness, the turkey has long since been a sandwich.

Christmas is over and is it not our experience that what remains is a Midnight Mass, a Communion, a memory of how the Crib looked as it was first seen, and the Christmas that was kept with and among the children? The tinsel and the cellophane are gone, the fuss is gratefully over; the Christmas with the kids still remains. Even in afterthought there is no weariness in what it meant to children.

And so, after the Mass and the Communion, of course, I do hope you all had children yelling around the place for Christmas. They are to be had in the world, and everybody seems to have turned to them. The organizations and societies, the Elks, the Chambers of Commerce, the K. of C., invited them in. I seem to recall something about theatre parties in the newspapers. The kids made sense out of public Christmas trees.

We had them in the parish as all parishes do. The schools bloomed with faces and rang with carols. And over and above the generality of children . . . children as such, so to speak . . . maybe you kept Christmas with sons and daughters, and nieces and nephews and cousins. I hope so. There is nothing like the twins, and Jackie, and Nancy and Patricia, and Jimmie and John David, all rushing in, it seems, in droves to make a Christmas. You may use any names you want for yourself . . . Mary and Bernard and Silvia and Mike, and Pietro and Stanislaus. But the kids make the Christmas, and I don't mean, quite, the Santa Claus part, and the sheer excitement that spreads like a young contagion, nor do I mean sentimentality and the vague good will hovering over the notion of Tiny Tim and the Dickens' "Christmas Carol." There is nothing wrong with that famous work except that it misses the reason for the point it makes. I don't mean the dreamy Spirit of Christmas Past, Present or Future with the holly and the plum pudding. I mean that the kids make Christmas in the sense of Christ Who is not the Spirit of Christmas, but the Fact of Christmas, Past, Present and to come.

That's why we turn to them at this season, and that's why we remember the children when the details of the occasion are all faded and stale. Christmas is the answer to children. Christmas is what we can take to them and from them and be glad . . . solid glad. Christmas speaks to every infant to tell what the infant is, and to every child to grant the child a name, no matter what he is otherwise called.

Look, it's like this. The key question in regard to Our Lord and the chief question in all the Gospel is the one that asks: *"What think you of Christ, whose son is He?"* You remember? There were various answers. But the real answer was that Christ is the Son of the Living God, True God and True Man. That is the basic fact He came to reveal. That is what makes Christmas, two thousand years after, because it made Christmas when the angels came, and Our Lady was young in the Motherhood of God.

Now, a paraphrase of that question asked of Christ is the basic question to be asked of all children and of every man. "Francis, and John, and Skippy, and Bill . . . whatever name you want . . . Thomas and Marty, whose son are you? To whom do you belong? Whose is the claim and the right and the ownership? Whence is the inheritance?" You see? That is the essential question, and the answer to it rises above anything that can ever be said to any child for this tells the household and the name.

So Christmas says: "You, child, Bernard or Elizabeth or Mary, you are not nameless. You are not a development in biology. You are not the accident of chance come of an untraceable ancestry.

You are not function or organization nor a bundle of mere cells set toward dissolution. Indeed, you are not."

And Christmas says: "You, child, William or Jerry or Paul, you are not limited even to whatever racial or national or family rights and gifts may or may not be your own. Actually your last name matters not."

And Christmas says . . . and with what clarity: "You, child— Louise, or Butch, or Elmer—you, child, are not the property of the State. Nor of Society either. You are not a ward, not you, child. The Kremlin is linked with the Father of Lies. That New Thought isn't even thought. That atom stuff means nothing. The Hygienists, the Sociologists, the Planned Parenters are wrong. Christmas says so. It does, child, and don't you be afraid."

For Christmas says: "You, kids, all of you, the blue-eyed, the stub-toed, the patched and the fur-coated, you, kids, belong to God, and God came to claim you when He found His Own Mother. That's what Christmas says. You are brothers to Christ and His heirs, and nobody owns you except God, Christ's Father, with Whom He as Son is equal, and by being Son He makes you sons. That is the measure of your inheritance. That is the sound of your name. You are, now and forever, because of Christmas, of the Household. Believe it, you belong. Christmas says so."

So there is something behind this instinct to run to children at Christmas. No wonder we remember that longest, and no wonder we remember that most fondly, even when the wreaths are withered and the ribbons frayed. The thing is buried in half our generation as almost a reflex action, almost a truth dimly remembered. But it is there. We confess it at this season. And it's just as well we think of it together with a Mass and a Communion, as the best of the day. For we were all kids. Somebody was glad for us once. And there is not a Mass that begins without saying: *"I will go unto the altar of God, to God Who giveth joy to my youth."*

THE TWENTY-FOUR HOURS

WHEN Father Hyland tasted the coffee the housekeeper had made for him, he knew that her cheerful "Good morning" had not been a happy accident. The strange, faintly uncomfortable feeling of being in another world, which had been with him since he had wakened, deepened and strengthened in his mind, almost to the edge of conviction. The coffee was hot and strong, as he liked it. Normally it would have been lukewarm and weak, as the Pastor liked it. She had been making it "for him that way for years and she was not going to fuss and bother over every assistant that happened to come along, and they could-either-drink-it-or-leave-it, for all she cared, for that's the way it poured out of the pot."

The priest was not moved to any personal affection by her sudden surrender. He still thought she was prejudiced, possessive, and puny in her virtuous soul, and he would always think so; but he resolved, without much effort at the moment, to say something pleasant should she pop through the door again. Perhaps he might even observe that it was a fine day. It was only his duty, and the coffee made it easy for once.

But then, he was lost in a further wonderment about the unusual crowds that had been at Mass on this winter week day, and at the marvelously increased numbers of the Communions. He lighted a cigarette and sipped half the coffee thinking about them. It was almost as good as a Holy Day. There was no occasion for it either, and there had not been confessions on the night before. Yet the crowds were there; nearly two railings had responded to the signal of the Non Sum Dignus bells.

Father Hyland was not alarmed at the Communions, even though there had been no confessions. He knew, as a priest, that hundreds of people, maybe most people, live good lives and are constantly eligible for daily Communion. It is merely that their love of God is not active enough that keeps them away. He was not scandalized; but he was certainly puzzled. What brought them so suddenly? What had happened in the night to get them all out of bed so early? And he discovered in his reflections that he had done rather better at his own Try on this day.

When Father Hyland was interiorly aware of the human effort in his priesthood, his mind spoke of the Mass as a Try. He said it now to himself: "Not a bad Try today, thank God." He had been recollected, much less scattered than usual, and even though his thoughts were running on the subject, he discovered that he could not remember any of the faces, or who was, or was not, at the rail. He had been utterly concentrated on the white Host his fingers had lifted from the golden ciborium so many, many times. He did not congratulate himself. He was grateful, but not in a mood to be pleased with himself for his success.

The housekeeper had inquired, Heavens, with a kind of music in her voice, if he would like another cup. "Yes," he said, "please, Margaret. And isn't this a fine day the Lord has given us?"

He turned to the morning paper, the sports pages first, of course. There was never any trouble on the sports pages. Lots of struggle, furious battles, much frenzy and exaggeration, and since he was a Twerp fan, much disappointment, but no troubles. Most priests love sports pages. The issues are not real: they are beautifully, and satisfactorily athletic only. Yes, the Twerps had lost again.

He glanced through most of the front-page headlines, and one or two of the feature stories before he noticed. The war news was vague and indecisive. There had been an accident on Route 5. . . . Johnny Gorman from St. Francis', apparently, had made it in time because the account related that the last rites were administered by a priest before the ambulance arrived from City Hospital. The Fire Department had been out in the night. But nowhere did the morning paper report a crime.

Father Hyland was down to the lesser matters now. Commissioner Fails to Accuse D. A. Expected Charges at Political Rally Unexploded. Mayor Says, "No Comment."

With the strange feeling of the early morning stronger than ever on him, Father Hyland wet his finger and turned the page. A boy from the public schools had beaten out a parochial school girl in the spelling contest. . . . Sister Emily won't like that. The Philharmonic announced a non-subscription Beethoven program for Friday night. The State had appropriated funds for that new mental out-patient clinic, at last . . . good thing too. But nowhere was there a new divorce announced; nowhere was there a case of a neglected child in court; nowhere did a young girl have a Narrow Escape. In the paper this morning no promise was made: Police to Double Prowl Cars.

It was not until Father Hyland read the advertisement for Medford's Department Store that the sweat stood out on his forehead, and his breath caught in his throat. The thing was a banner, run in under the Medford insignia at the top of the ad. It was in bold letters and it dominated the page.

PRICES CUT ON BOYS' SUITS. 20% REDUCED

Due to a discovery made late last night, Scuffo-Brand-Boys'-Clothes are found to be one-quarter wool, and not one-half wool as advertised in listing already gone to press.

PRICES REDUCED: 20% OFF
MEDFORD'S . . . FIRST WITH THE TRUTH!

With his hand trembling, the priest searched. He *tried* to find a report of violence in the night, he *tried* to find a report of a crime . . . even a little crime, a misdemeanor even. The paper yielded nothing, and he pushed back his chair in a rush. His heart beat within him. He would phone Johnny Gorman to ask if he had noticed anything in this day. He would call right away. But before he burst through the door to run up the stairs, he paused to crush the cigarette in the ash tray. Not in a saucer. In the cigarette tray. The housekeeper was annoyed, poor Margaret, when she found cigarette butts soaking in the saucers.

A courteous, pleasant voice answered at St. Francis' and told him that "all the priests were in the church for a funeral Mass, but Father Gorman would return about 10:30," and "Would you want to leave your number for a return call at that time?" Father Hyland said a quiet "No, thank you."

At 10:35 he rang St. Francis' again. "Johnny," he shouted, "Johnny, do you notice anything funny about today? I mean, have you felt any difference in things?"

There was silence on the wire. Father Hyland waited for his friend and classmate to answer. "Look, Hy," came the answer, "look, Hy, you all right?"

It developed after a while that Father John Gorman had noticed nothing, nothing at all . . . except that the corpse at the funeral had had quite a lot of mourners in the church . . . a mean old guy too . . . and except that . . .

"Oh, Hy, you'll get a kick out of this. The altar boy spilled the incense, and the Old Man didn't say a word. Not a word . . ."

After Father Hyland had subsided in his leather chair, the whole communication seemed normal, routine, and as it always was with Johnny. Except . . . except . . . it could be. . . .

He checked the time on his watch and turned the switch on his radio. It was the hour for the 10:45 news broadcast.

"Again, ladies and gentlemen, we bring you the Up-to-the-Minute News Hour sponsored by the Gem, the Up-to-the-Minute Theatre in the Heart of Downtown Milton. . . . The indecisive war news from the Eastern Arctic area, as reported by the wire services earlier today, has now definitely cleared. According to a dispatch just in from General MacSweeney's headquarters, three of our medical units have been sent into the ruined city of Soul with huge supplies of blood plasma. The dispatch, dated shortly after midnight, last night, emphasizes that the blood is to be used on enemy troops. No casualties have been reported since yester-day. It is expected that the city of Soul will soon be regained."

Father Hyland argued with himself that his pulse should be pounding. It should be pounding like a hammer beating on nails, but instead, he found himself calm, half smiling, indeed, he said to himself in his thoughts: "I am serene."

The priest listened to some minor and unimportant news coming over the air, and then the eager voice of the announcer broke through sharply again.

"Flash! We have just had it confirmed by Washington that the city of Soul has been retaken, and that the earlier medical campaign implemented by General MacSweeney has met complete success. The War Department announces that enemy troops following three American units loaded with blood plasma have replied vigorously to our attack with gifts of caviar. Flash! Caviar is a specially prepared food delicacy, and the War Department repeats: all counter-attack as of this morning was by caviar on toasted bread. Experts here predict, ladies and gentlemen, that this could possibly mean the beginning of the Peace."

Father Hyland had given up trying to make ordinary sense out of this day, its events, its coffee, or its revolution in himself. The thing made sense, all right, but not ordinary sense, not natural sense. "The whole day is super," he said, and he said it aloud. "It's absolutely super!"

The announcer was apologizing for the necessity of going so quickly into the commercial, and also, he said, for the length of the commercial. "But . . . but . . . The Gem, the Up-to-the-Minute Theatre in the Heart of Downtown Milton has changed the movie program for today. It's not sensational, folks, it's not colossal. The management of the Gem, however, has asked me to say it's super. *Furious Passion*, the feature scheduled for today has been cancelled. In place of *Furious Passion* the management has booked as a special attraction, Will Bizney's new cartoon feature with symphonic music: *Not of This World*. We repeat, special attraction for today . . . *Not of This World*. The B Picture, originally scheduled for all performances, has been cancelled. Today there will be no B Picture. This is the Up-to-the-Minute News Fifteen Minutes, sponsored by the Gem, the Up-to-the-Minute Theatre, still in the Heart of Downtown Milton, folks, still in the Heart of Downtown Milton. . . .

As he put on his black overcoat, brushed his black hat, and walked down the stairs, Father Hyland was fearful of what he would see. Crushing the thin ice on the driveway as he walked to the garage, the priest could observe no change in the world as he had always known it. The sky was blue, yet there was a threat of more snow in the clouds to the North. No angels sang in the air: only the frost. No flambeaux blazed from the sun. The time was still winter, and the sun was only the sun. He had turned the handle of his Chevvy door, and had started into the car when he saw a plain, ordinary fact. The front left tire was flat.

The kids, out in the schoolyard for an official breath of fresh air, came over to help him jack the automobile up and change to the spare. He looked closely at the four of them and they were laughing as if they were glad to be jacking up an automobile and changing a tire under his direction. It was normal with the kids too. No change here. Nothing altered. After he had told them to "get back there now, and see that you know your catechism when I come in this afternoon," he waved gaily at them, and stepped on the starter.

Ah! It turned the motor over in spite of the cold. He must remember to pay his garage bill today. That mechanic had done a good job on the distributor.

His notion as he steered down the drive for the hospital calls was that the kids probably wouldn't know their religious lesson this afternoon. They'd forget what he had told them last week. As usual.

All the cars on the streets were moving slowly, sanely. When he paused at the boulevard Stop sign, the lady on the street to the right waved him on. She was driving a Cadillac. He also noted Al McGumption, the cop, at the corner of Main Street. Al had his arms folded across his chest, and he looked pleased as a Guardian Angel out of a job.

The rest of the day glided over him in the same way. It was super: super, but normal. No bands played in the parks. Choral Clubs did not suddenly serenade the neon signs with Christmas carols. The neons were all mercifully unlit, in the daylight anyway. As he passed the Pool Parlors, he could see that the gang had not congregated at the windows to watch the girls crossing Laurel Street in the wind. Nowhere in his travels could he find people excitedly discussing the war news he had heard on the radio.

In the hospital, at two house calls, in the bank, at the barbershop, everybody was silent. He was silent too. It occurred to him that it would not be quite Christian to mention that we had been Christian about the blood plasma, and perhaps the enemy would prefer no publicity about the caviar. What your left hand did was no business of your right hand . . . not if there was to be Peace. All day long Father Hyland was himself silent about the war, and the news, and the day, and the change, which was subtle, simple . . . and inner.

He was glad to observe, though, that the Gem Theatre in the Heart of Downtown Milton opened to heavy trade. People needed gaiety, and they needed a diversion, especially with music and color and innocence. If *Not of This World* stayed on till his day off, he might go to watch it.

Late in the afternoon, after the kids in the weekly religion class had failed again, but only in the language for the knowledge he tried to give them, Father Hyland made a last stop at the house of Mrs. Straub. "Did he come home with drink on him again?" he asked, and Mrs. Straub smiled and admitted that he had.

"But, Father," she said, "he wasn't loaded. It was only a faint breath. Beer, I think. He walked straight in, patted little Elsie's head, and gave her a sweater he had bought. And he had a new suit from Medford's too, for Jimmie. Then he kissed me on the forehead and told me the food I provided was fit for a king. Later, I heard him humming. Poor fellow, he's asleep now, but I mean to wake him when the Twerps play television at nine."

Father Hyland's own dinner, when he got to it, seemed both copious and savory. He swapped Seminary stories with the pastor. He was grateful for food, clean linen, silver spoons, and the way the mind of man had invented a fork. He asked the pastor if he didn't think they had a fine parish in a fine city, in a fine world. The pastor nodded calmly in his usual wisdom.

The priest was upstairs again in the room with the telephone attachment, in the room where he had listened to the radio that morning. He sat in his chair with a sigh of contentment, and slapped open the evening paper. There on the outside page of the evening paper was a great, black headline stretched across the top:

THOU SHALT LOVE THE LORD THY GOD WITH THY WHOLE HEART, WITH THY WHOLE SOUL, AND WITH THY WHOLE MIND; AND THOU SHALT LOVE THY NEIGHBOR AS THYSELF.

Such had been Father Hyland's experience during the Twenty-Four Hours that he did not think the headline strange. He merely thought it a good headline. Normal. Proper. Under it were two words: **GOOD NEWS.**

As he read the details, thinking that soon he must pause to say his beads for his Mother's Son's sake, Father Hyland was pleased and interested to note that the entire front page was given over to the complete text of the Sermon on the Mount.

———————

Father Hyland had confidently expected that he would awake the next morning feeling like an angel, but he was chagrined and disturbed that his exhausted soul had not perceived the first summons of his alarm clock, and that he had to rush to be on time for his Mass. The boys in the sacristy were noisy as he came in a few minutes late. He told them rather sharply to make sure the candles were lighted, and the wine and water were ready. It took effort to pull his mind back to the prayer for the amice. Worse than that, he discovered he was more curious than pious as his eyes wandered out to the pews in a swift attempt to see if the crowds had returned. They had not.

At about the Offertory, after the sections of the Mass that change each day had all been read, and he had come again to the Ordinary with the familiar prayers that never change, he was aware of serious inattention in his mind. The Twenty-four Hours, actually, had become a distraction. He was not easy within himself, and he was not completely in control of his own love of God. The Mass, almost from the beginning to the end, could only be described as a Try. He tried, but humanly he felt he did not achieve. The people at the communion rail were the same ones that came every morning, and not numerous.

The thanksgiving afterward was most difficult of all. He had to wrestle and spiritually to demand. What had happened? Could it be that he had merely dreamed? Was the brief Golden Age but a figment of his desires? Could this be the wish of his heart making pictures for his mind because he wanted charity to be easy? Did he, unconsciously, want to put the whole burden on God's grace, as though it still would be grace if the world were *forced?* Or had the Twenty-four Hours really occurred as an actual experience out of all the unimaginable eons since Creation? Did this day stand there in time like a secret, like a Paradise to be remembered forever as Eden is remembered? What . . .

The speed that carried Father Hyland through the kitchen door of the rectory was as angelic as earthbound, sacerdotal feet may attain. If his cassock caught at his heels on the stairs, if he made a clatter at doors and at the turnings on the first floor, and the second floor, he did not notice. The newspapers! The newspapers in his room with the evidence of print! Where were they?

"Margaret," he called down in a roar, "Margaret, what in the world happened to yesterday's newspapers? They were right here last night!"

She had followed his rush to the foot of the stairs, and now she countered his insistence. "They are not in the world at all; I burned the morning paper as I have been told to do, and I burned the evening paper, as I have been told to do. I keep a neat house, as I have also been told to do! If you are in such a hurry for the news why don't you turn on the radio?"

Father Hyland did. "This is the Gem Theatre Early News Hour bringing you the war news of the moment. . . . In spite of fierce resistance reported in all sectors, six units of our troops have advanced in a new attack begun at midnight last night. . . . The F. B. I. disclose new violations of security codes. . . . Feature Attraction today at the Gem Theatre in the Heart of Downtown Milton . . . *Furious Passion*. . . .

The priest switched off the machine, and slowly, slowly descended to his breakfast. Margaret looked at him in slanted silence as she put down his coffee and moved the ash tray nearer.

"But what could it have been?" his mind kept searching. "Could that gesture with the ash tray be significant? Was *she* keeping this a secret as the whole world would now keep it a secret? Would all the papers be gone . . . by a Plan? Would all trace, all record, all memory be destroyed by Providence so that only the personal heart would remember? Or was it a dream after all?"

He sipped the coffee tentatively. It was lukewarm and weak. But he pulled the ashtray nearer, and with resolute purpose. With a willed, genuine blow for Peace, he carefully, minutely knocked off the gray flakes of ashes. "Sackcloth and ashes," he thought. Then he lifted his voice in the direction of the kitchen door, "Margaret, it's a fine day the Lord has given us today. . . ."

JANUARY FIRST

THIS is the financial season, open season for the decimal point, the month when the pastor goes into the strenuous conference with his books and comes to the pulpit, one Sunday morning, with the first precious copy of his Annual Report. This too is the season of revelations, the hour of facts, for commonly the Annual Report is accompanied by the list of contributors in support of the parish, a catalogue compiled with loving care, within which every pastor dreads even the shadow of a fraction of error.

Now, the financial report is a matter of business, of Church law, and episcopal direction. It is a phase of pastoral duty, and will be issued this year, as in the past, no matter what is written anywhere about it. This being the time, and finances being a wintry Catholic concern, we may venture on a few considerations, for, believe it or not, there are a few considerations not elaborated in the usual pastor's "talk about money." Not many perhaps, but then again, perhaps quite a few.

We could, for instance, be confused about the fiscal side of parish life and come to see it as entirely divorced from the spiritual. We could fall into the error that a priest on a sick call is properly employed, but that a priest mentioning a collection has somehow descended from his high vocation. We could miss the halo over the basket, fail to see the sanctity of the accounts, and regard Catholicism as a Faith that is compromised by any crass, unworthy and rude association with a bank. But the exact reverse is true.

The material can become spiritual even though the spiritual can never become material. The pastor preaches the lessons of Christ to his people; he instructs children in Christ; he offers the Holy Sacrifice; watches for the sick, is available for confessions, sees to it that the school is in proper operation, remembers the poor: but the preaching could not be in an empty lot, the children cannot be gathered in a cellar, the Sacrifice requires a decent place, the school requires a faculty, equipment, and heated classrooms.

Whosoever commands the end, commands the necessary means to obtain the end. It is Our Lord Who commissioned the daily parish life in the Faith and, therefore, it is Our Lord Who sends the priest on his task of writing out the new envelope list and adding up the old. The parish business is just as spiritual a matter as a sick call. I do not mean to imply an eighth sacrament, the financial one, nor would you read these remarks correctly if you judged that there are no grades possible within the spiritual, and that a collection ranks with a Retreat. But what is said is that money matters are not outside the pale, that they belong within the category of the spiritual, and that a priest has lost none of his dignity in the cultivation of the ability to add.

The Church, itself, has taught this in the formulation of the 5th ecclesiastical commandment. The support of the parish church has not been left as a matter of choice, but within one's own means and proportionately, it is of obligation. Collections are concerns of conscience.

Possibly all this is a rare and exotic worry in the traditional examination of sins before night prayers. Probably there are only a few sensitive souls who are grieved to remember that a quarter was not a half dollar. Certainly no missioner that I ever heard in a pulpit was prepared with a sermon on the vice of fiscal neglect, and quite obviously, the pastor, wise man that he is, depends on parish pride, good will, and his own exquisite diplomacy. But the actual basis of his confidence in the presence of bills is the sheer duty accepted by his people from a church law.

The distressing thought occurs that these pages make painful and arduous reading and that nobody has persevered to the present paragraph depth. However, that is a risk which any paragraph runs, so let us loosen the purse strings and go on in reckless comfort.

The parish church, to all purposes, belongs to the people. It is not the pastor's personal property, nor the Bishop's, nor does the structure belong to the trustees who would not know what to do with it in any case. Beyond the legal forms of incorporation and the niceties of law, the parish church belongs to the families who live, religiously, under its roof. They built it, maintain it, are married and buried before its altar; their children are baptized in it, their visits to Our Lord are made in it, and they sit pretty much in the same pews for a lifetime. They decorate it for Christmas and Easter, pass it on the way to work, and listen to the sound of its bells.

A parish church is identified with names and faces, with flesh and blood people, and they, in any real sense, own it. Hence the democracy of the Annual Report. When debt is decreased or surplus accumulated, the parish families experience the beautiful glow of gain. The Report is like a summary of a household budget, and the people are really more interested in it than the priest. It answers the question: "How are we doing?" It answers that question much more than it replies to the question: "How's he doing?"

───────────

And in that companion to the Annual Report, the list of individual donors, it may appear that the larger contributors have spent more than the lesser ones. But again the reverse is true. The list is an account of investors, and the larger donors have put away more than the lesser donors. It works, of course, in proportion to means, and big figures do not always indicate big investment. But any money that vanishes in a collection basket is not lost or squandered or wasted in riotous living. It has been put away where *"thieves do not break in and steal."*

An old story is told of Wendell Phillips, the famous minister, which seems strange to me, for such narratives more usually have as their hero a Father Burke or a Father Higgins. On the occasion of the special collection, Dr. Phillips is supposed to have read the text about the Lord returning gifts "*a hundred fold.*" He then went on to say: "Gentlemen, you have heard the terms. If you are satisfied with the security, put down the cash." The story concludes, as such stories do, in triumph. The collection was the biggest ever.

Lastly, we may well wonder if there be any soul who, upon discovering in a list how much he gave over a year, would declare in firm resolution to himself: "This must stop. This must not go on. This wild prodigality must cease." Do you suppose anyone has ever worried over *this* dissipation, gone sleepless over *this* excess?

YOU CAN'T SAY YOU CAN'T

ATTENTION should forthrightly be aimed at two elements in the practice of the Catholic Faith which can give both zest and continuity to prayers, and also, what I can only term a sense of incessant campaign. There is no use in searching for something to give a feeling of success, for prayer is the one human activity where any inner suggestion of triumph, any shy satisfaction is most likely to be false. But zest and continuity are other matters entirely, and an awareness of a planned, strategic, and undeviating effort can be spiritually invigorating and morally encouraging. Most people discover that not the least difficulty in prayers is to avoid feeling scattered.

Now the very first help is the simple factor of time. Time, although the philosophers declare it to be completely distinct from eternity, is certainly an available instrument for reaching to the Eternal. A lack of judicious observation of the clock can hobble and halt many an honest attempt to pray sincerely, for the energies are left uncommanded, and the will is wasted on the unspecific path of mere desire. Of course it is possible to pray all the time. Saints have done so, and some folk who would be horrified to think themselves saintly live in an almost continuous consciousness of God. Furthermore, a voluntary dedication, a daily assignment of all work and play and activity for the glory of God can make anything genuine prayer whether it is digging ditches, doing the dishes, selling insurance, or even playing golf, which is often the same as digging ditches except that the work is not done in a straight line. Anything can be prayer.

And yet, for most people, an eye on the clock can give a powerful spurt, and a welcome signal for praying that is quite other than the ear on the alarm clock which shocks us into rising. Those who live in monasteries and convents, the professional pray-ers, so to speak, those whose vocation it is to struggle constantly to be with God, spend much of their efforts with a Breviary, or the Divine Office. Another name for this ceaseless, liturgical prayer is the Hours.

The Book into which the psalms, and the Scriptures, and the lessons are collected is actually called a Book of Hours. In it there are prayers for Matins, or morning, and prayers for Prime, Tierce, Sext, and None, which plainly are, in English, First, Third, Sixth and Ninth . . . *hours*. The day is thus bent into an arch of hours. It becomes a schedule, an order. The Church is fully convinced of the value of specific time in the spiritual campaigns. But that should not surprise us since from childhood we have been bidden to Morning Prayers and Night Prayers, and we have been counselled by the catechism to pray at "times of temptation," and at "times of trial."

I remember with profit a good Sister who, during her life, was teacher and friend to thousands of school children. She taught for a full and happy career, and was known in religion as Sister Mary Bernard of the Congregation of St. Joseph. However, to her numerous alumnae and alumni, I am sure she is remembered as Sister Mary Bernard of the Eighth Grade. During the vacation seasons she was ardently devoted to travel, and I hope it is no violation of convent dignity were I to reveal that, among the nuns, Sister Mary Bernard, because of her holiday achievements, was known as Sister Mary Go.

In her classroom there was always a big clock located, usually on the top of the piano. When the clock struck the hour, Sister Mary Bernard was wont to say: "Children?" And the students, knowing full well what was meant, would reply to the gong: "Glory be to the Father, and to the Son, and to the Holy Ghost." They studied, did Sister Bernard's pupils, but when the clock told the time, they prayed: every hour, on the hour. I am certain that hundreds of men and women who may have forgotten compound fractions, now have no difficulty in praying whatsoever, for their effort is geared to time.

Then there were the heroic nuns who staffed the kitchen and the laundry at Niagara years ago. They were French Canadians and they loved God by peeling potatoes, washing socks, and baking bread for the college. It was an occupation which, obviously, required a constant attention to the hours of the day. Ask any mother, housewife, or cook. All over their quarters, and in every place of labor, every clock had a sign on it, and the sign said in French: "Stop. Think of God." It's that element of time again, you see.

Certainly these Sisters got tired. Certainly they became distracted, and in spite of the reminder on the clocks, sometimes found meager eloquence in their prayers. So they all had a wonderful and sovereign method to match the challenge of the signs. The first was to say very simply to God: "Whatever. Whenever." Do I need to translate and give the full phrase? It was: "Whatever You want, dear God, and whenever You want me to do it."

The other method of the kitchen Sisters must have been superbly effective for them when their nerves were frayed, and their fingers worn, and when their poor holy backs ached with the sanctity of their lives. It is a kind of an oblique prayer, a prayer at one remove. I am utterly sure that the Sisters would think of this method only out of their humility, but for the rest of us it may be very necessary. The good Sister would *not* say to her soul. "I want to love God." When she was tired and empty of any consolation, she said: "I want to want to love God." I venture not into the realm of the theologian or the ascetic, but it seems to me that "to want to want to love God," is pretty wonderful: and enormously useful as a prayer for any soul.

The last neglected element in the effort to pray which ought to be mentioned now is the sense of Company. You know, without any danger of boasting or complacency, without any temptation to shift a burden to others, the plain fact of the matter is that we Catholics are never alone. We are not isolated souls, singular, lonely, celled and engaged in a solitary effort. We are members of a great Company, and whether we think of it or not, we pray in Company. There is not the least Our Father or the faintest Ave that is not joined in its flight to God with millions of others. To be Catholic is to be in the midst of a vast chorus, to be joined in perpetual choir, to be linked and bonded and accompanied. This is the tremendous social doctrine called the Communion of Saints, but in the attempt to pray, I prefer to think of it as a sense of Company.

Some of the mission societies have published a chart that tells the hours of Mass all over the world and suggests that no moment of the day passes except that Mass be offered somewhere. And thus saying the grace for your dinner, casting a swift prayer at a temptation, kneeling at 4 A.M., tipping your hat in front of a church are all done in the spiritual company of a priest, perhaps in China, or on an island in the sea, who is beginning the prayers that are the preface to the unending Sacrifice offered from "*the rising of the sun to the going down thereof.*" I argue that this is an encouraging coincidence and a definite help to any man. It is true of any moment in the day, and the knowledge can serve to reinforce the straggling, thin, and feeble effort of any soul. How can a man be convinced of his own incompetency when he prays not alone but in the great Crowding that is the Church.

Lastly, the Company is not limited to earth, but includes the Saints in the presence of God, St. Joseph, and the Holy Mother of God, which is part of the reason why the doctrine is called the Communion of Saints. There is no flattery here for us, you know. And most people find that there is strength in the thought of the Saints joining us, because prayer with and through the Saints and Our Lady is a partial meaning of what Christ implied when He said: "*Where two or three are gathered together in My name, there am I in the midst of them.*"

There are dozens of prayers that are said in Our Lady's Company, and one of them, the Memorare, is said in the Company of both Our Lady and St. Bernard. But here is one that may be said in the Company of Our Lady and the little child from whom it first came.

When you need something very urgently from God, when your petition presses on your heart, and you want to cry out, then pray with Our Lady confidently summoned to be near. She is very powerful, the Mother of God, and she is very knowing, and sensitive, and very understanding. Once she prayed water into wine. So you ask her help in your need, and you pray:

> You can't say you can't.
> You won't say you won't.
> Please, dear Mother, say you will. *Amen.*

THE DAY OF THE MAGI

It so happened that the feast of the Epiphany fell on the day that the religious instruction classes resumed after the Christmas recess. If it also happened that you were standing in a hidden place in the church, behind a pillar, let us say, or back of the evergreens still surrounding the Crib to the right of the altar, you would have heard the valiant efforts of the Sister trying to translate the ancient Greek word to a significance that would fit into the minds of her Fourth Graders. "Epiphany," said the Sister, "means a showing forth, and the feast remembers the very first discovery of Christ by people who were not His Own, that is, who were not of Israel." The class remained passive: they were not ready to crown the Three Kings.

The Sister drew a deep breath and struggled after the Star: "The Epiphany probably did not occur until the Christ was over a month old, but our Faith has always kept the feast on January 6th, and today, children, is January 6th." The benches were still passive, and an implicit and unfavorable impression seemed to fill the church that January 6th was not much of a date to have a feast on. "People talk of them as Kings," the Sister elaborated, with discipline in her eyes, "and the pretty cards picture them as Kings. But they were really Magi. Magi are Wise Men. They watch stars." The discipline in her eyes was imperative: the class sat silent before the information. "These Magi-Wise Men were looking for the King, and they found Him on this day, and that is why some people call the Epiphany, 'Little Christmas.'"

This was something different. Little Christmas. A stir of definite interest became sibilant through the class. Heads looked up. Light gleamed in the lifted faces. Christmas, big or little, was an event they could not, and would not, neglect. Christmas had come and gone, but here was a remnant they had missed, a recurring magic, a satisfaction not often to be gained in the world of approach, possession, and inevitable loss. Even though "little," today was "Christmas" again.

"Yes, Little Christmas," the Sister repeated, encouraged as she was, and then went on to tell the story of the search, the Star, the visit to Herod, the advice of the scholars, and the last hastening jog of the camels on the road to Bethlehem. "And there in Mary's arms, and with St. Joseph standing near and giving his permission, the Magi looked upon the face of the Child, and fell on their knees to the floor for joy of Him."

Eloquence came to the Sister, and out of her love and her need to tell what she knew, she harked back to her convent chapel where the Epiphany is observed as a great and solemn feast, higher in rank than even Christmas itself. "Really," she said, "this was the First Benediction ever given on earth. Our Lady's hands made the First Monstrance to hold the Christ for people to see. Our Lady is called the 'House of Gold,' and on Epiphany her hands were like gold enclosing Him to hold Him up over the heads of the Wise Men. Joseph was the acolyte, the great, strong acolyte who raised the torches that were like candles . . . because it was night, children. It had to be in the night because the Magi could see the Star. And the Magi, the Wise Men, were kneeling just as we kneel at Benediction. And children, there was incense there too, for one of the gifts they made was incense, frankincense. It was the First Benediction ever . . ."

But the children were lost again. They had subsided and the light was gone from their faces. They had never *been* to Benediction, and their experience with religion did not include so wondrous and vivid a ceremony as the Eucharistic Blessing for Epiphany, Feast of the First Class, in a convent chapel. Little Christmas, yes: Benediction, not yet.

"Look, it was this way," said the Sister, inspired to action, and she swooped to the Crib to the right of the altar and made bold to extract, bodily, the plaster figures of the Kings, the camel, and the dark servant holding the lead rope for the camel. She deposited her armful of Magi, the servant, the beast of burden on the flat top of the altar rail, far to the left. "Look," she repeated, "these are the poor Men, way out here. They want to find the Christ Child, and Mary, but they are miles away in a desert." This was more like it, the class declared by its deep attention. This was more like it, and the marble railing turned to desert sand, the mere yards of space, to miles, and it did not matter that two of the Three Kings were apparently making the whole journey on their plaster knees. "A week passed," the Sister explained, "and now they are here." She cautiously moved the figures a distance to the right. "Another week passed, poor Men, and now they are here." Fully half of the altar railing had now been achieved, and, as the Magi moved, the Sister's caution changed to enthusiasm, and when the Crib was in reach, to downright triumph. She flicked the switch that turned on the Star over the Manger, and in a last burst of education, set the Magi, the servant and the camel where they belonged, inside the Christmas roof, at their rightful places on the straw. "You see," she said, "they made it. Epiphany means that Wise Men searched . . . and won."

The Fourth Graders were delighted. They liked anybody winning. They flocked over in a group and knelt on the steps outside the railing to peer into the Magi Goal of the Christmas Crib, and to confirm with their own eyes that the Wise Men were there. They smiled in satisfaction, and in a just and simple congratulation to the ancient Kings.

Their instructor and guide sighed the ancient sigh of the teacher and gazed on them all with fondness, but, no doubt, it never occurred to her that she was as *"the chief priests and scribes of the people,"* placed by St. Matthew's Gospel in the court of Herod. Yet she was as the *"chief priests and the scribes"* for she had found an answer to give to a question, and a journey's end to a search. It was: *"Bethlehem of Juda."*

One of the Fourth Graders suddenly was bright with knowledge. "I know why it's Little Christmas, Sister. They brought presents."

The Sister was stern with discipline. "Yes," she answered, "presents of gold, myrrh and frankincense . . . incense, as at Benediction."

"THE DAY OF THE MEETING"

No GREAT erudition is required at this season of the year to predict that, come a cold February day, the newspapers will carry an article about the ground hog seeing his shadow, with, perhaps a cartoon showing a little man ruefully facing the rest of the winter with a shawl wrapped around his neck. We do not need to know where the old legend about the shadow came from, and certainly there is no harm in it. The day provides a pale sort of joke. It's one of those tales, like the Easter bunny, that you tell to children. February 2nd is Ground-hog Day.

But here, as in so many other matters, the poor, deprived, feeble imagination of the world has to be content with a mere story, with a small and empty tradition, and with a ritual without much meaning, while burning in the centuries is the great, blazing, glorious fire of the Faith. Ground-hog Day, indeed. The rite of seeing a shadow, indeed. February 2nd is a Feast Day of Our Lady! It marks the first journey she ever made with the Child in her arms. This is the fortieth day since Christmas. The Armenians called it "The Coming of the Son of God to the Temple." The Greeks called it "The Day of the Meeting." And if we think of it in terms of the lovely ritual, in terms of the delicate and graceful ceremony in sanctuaries of the Faith, this day is Candlemas Day.

I am reminded of those lines of John Keats in the "Ode on a Grecian Urn": "Beauty is truth, truth beauty,—that is all ye know on earth, and all ye need to know." I am reminded of them, not so much for the Keats conclusion about what we are able to know on earth, but rather for the rich and blessed direction of the Faith which is forever leading us to the beauty in truth, and to the truth in beauty. Inside of Catholicism the identity is valid. Keats was right: beauty is truth and truth beauty, because they are both faint and far reflections of God, and the Faith is constantly enchanting, feeding, delighting, ennobling the mind in the contemplation of them.

It is difficult to be a Catholic and to be dull of soul. We never ought to be bored; we live in a Faith that sings as it teaches, colors as it makes clear, entrances as it guides, charms the heart as it strengthens the will, that leads us through beauty as it moves us to truth.

This is only one instance, but, come, let us look at the Feast of February 2nd. The day is forty days beyond Bethlehem, and that brings up the whole preparation for the birth of Christ. This day is so because the Mosaic Law required that the mother of a first-born son wait that length of time and then come with the child to the Temple. Our Lady, the world's one exception to the fact of sin, did not exempt herself from the Law of Moses. So we see her now walking on the road, quiet, with a virginal grace about her, moving on towards the Temple of the God of Jacob and Isaac, and carrying in her arms the God of Jacob and Isaac, and of all the world.

This is the first journey of Christ on the earth. This is the first extension of Bethlehem beyond the little hillside. There will be a flight soon, an excursion, so to speak, made in fear to a foreign land, but Our Lady knows nothing of that now. She has not heard of sorrow yet.

Then the moment comes when she is within the great Temple gates and within the broad paved court, and although there are crowds about her, she is still alone for she brings here the Reason why these courts and stones were laid.

There is a brief ceremony and she surrenders Him to a stranger for the first time. Old Simeon finds her and sees what he prayed to see. "*Now Thou dost dismiss Thy servant, O Lord, according to Thy word in peace. Because my eyes have seen Thy salvation, which Thou hast prepared before the face of all peoples: a light to the revelation of the Gentiles, and the glory of Thy people Israel.*"

His words are not lost, for the Church has taken this prayer to close each day. This is the night-prayer of the Faith.

The woman named Anna, unknown to history except for her sanctity, her grief over a husband lost in death, and for her sudden appearance here in the Temple, salutes Our Lady with a wordless cry. She is the voice of the Temple, articulation for the pavements and the great stones, and she makes the courtyards, the roofs, the wide bronze doors ring with the meaning of another Visitation. Her cry is the Temple speaking: "*Whence is this to me that the mother of my Lord should come to me?*" And then Our Lady with the Child has moved away, and the Temple is silent again. What was to be, now is, and what is to come has been foreshadowed. Mary has learned of a sword, and of a sorrow, and has felt the first distant quaking of His Calvary.

Beauty? So much that the breath is caught in the contemplation of it, and it rests on the heart like a pain. What story or romance or poetry holds so much? What imagining, what wishful musing or dreaming or thinking can match this? Where is the parallel for this anywhere in human literature? This single scene, this Day of the Meeting, this February 2nd focus of the Faith, this setting and theme for the Mass and the liturgy of a single day contains more within its commas, or in its least caesura, than is caught to lyric in great poetry.

But the Faith has not concluded. This is true! This is real! This is only part, episode, and fragment of a whole reality, a whole glorious fact. "Beauty is truth, truth beauty," and the full thrill in Catholicism is that they are one, they are not separate, they do blend and fuse and become identified. That's the whole point. In the Faith we are not looking at make-believe. This has happened. Our Lady did come and with her was the Child. All we do now is remember.

The Church lets us move beyond our wonder, and gives us language and sign to tell our happiness. Candles, pure, white, beeswax candles are brought to our sanctuary as Christ was brought to the Temple. We bless them, and dedicate them to God. They are lighted and carried in procession, and then they are set to stand above our altars, above our linen, and our chalice, while the Faith goes on to other scenes, and to other days beyond this time of Candlemas.

CONVERTS

ONE of the very happy and satisfactory tasks of the priesthood is the instruction of prospective converts in the elements of the Catholic Faith. I do not mean preaching from a pulpit, nor lecturing to students in a school, nor even the conduct of catechism classes, but something quite different, the instruction of adults, one by one, through a series of appointments scheduled in the office of the Rectory of the local parish church.

This is work that is unpublicized, that is unobserved, perhaps unknown to most Catholics, but it is going on all the time. Most priests are constantly engaged in it, and have a list of people to instruct individually once or twice a week. The number will fluctuate according as the grace of God works and as Catholic people give good example. Sometimes a priest will have two or three to plan for through the evenings of a week, and then suddenly the list will grow and he is busy every evening and many afternoons with eight or ten or more candidates. There are few seasons of the year when he will have no such engagements, but the revelation I would make is that all this is very normal and usual and, indeed, routine.

People are coming into the Faith all the time. Now and again when some public figure, some person of notable achievement is received into the Church, the action will get mentioned in the news, but these are the exceptions. Usually it is not news except to the individual, his family, perhaps his neighborhood, and certainly to the priest who gives the instructions. To him it is ranked with the best news of the year, for it is the "good news" of Our Lord coming to a human soul.

You see, it is not possible to become a Catholic simply by raising the hand in a determined manner and saying "count me in." I do not mean to imply that any long, difficult or arduous course in theoretical theology is required, or that a convert must qualify as a sort of religious Einstein, but the Church does demand a definite and practical instruction in the Creed, in the Sacraments, and in the Moral Law. A man must know about the Faith before he can say either yes or no to it.

Catholicism is not merely an attitude, not merely an association, and above all it is not a pious emotion. There is a substance to the Faith, a content out of which comes a rule of life and a method for reaching God, and the only way to discover what the content holds is through personal instructions fitted to the individual. Hence the appointments and the work of the priest in the local parish.

But where do the converts come from and who are they? I am sure any priest in any parish would reply that they come from everywhere and that they are nearly everybody. Young and old, men and women, from every non-Catholic religion on the modern scene, and a huge number with no religion at all. They are the rich and the poor, High School graduates and college graduates and people who never had much to do with books. They are mothers and fathers of children, and the children themselves. They are G. I.'s, septuagenarians, people who ought to be Catholic, people who have waited years to do this, and people who have just had a bright idea. Some know about Our Lady of Fatima, and some have never heard of Our Lady. Some have been to Christmas Midnight Mass, and some have never seen a priest close-up in their lives. They come from small towns and villages, and they come from the big cities. Some want to keep the instructions going till they exhaust the libraries, and some want to finish the course as quickly as possible, and about nine-tenths of them find the experience one of the most interesting they have ever had.

Are most converts involved in a mixed marriage or in a romance with a Catholic? The answer to that one is "yes" if you extend the terms to include all manner of association with good Catholics. Of course the answer is "yes": how in the nature of human living could it be otherwise? There has to be a point at which the Faith is touched. There has to be an original bond, or introduction to the Church, and by far the usual introduction is the human association. It often occurs in a marriage, even after many years. It often occurs through a romance where Catholic boy meets non-Catholic girl, or Catholic girl meets non-Catholic boy. It also happens through bridge clubs, basketball games, bowling leagues, business offices, and through living on the same street and borrowing a snow shovel. There is no telling how it may happen, but it happens most often through the contagion of the Catholic Faith in, among, through and by people. Father Thomas Merton apparently found the Faith in books and through the unhappiness of his life; Arnold Lunn found the Faith by trying to debate against it; Mrs. Claire Luce found the Faith, as she has written, through sorrow and distress; Mr. Budenz re-discovered the Faith through failure of his communism, but most people find the Faith through knowing, loving, observing or being associated with Catholics.

Easily enough that brings up the chances and the opportunities in ordinary life, and I mean, bluntly, your ordinary life. Most Catholics try to lean over backward lest they be guilty of "influencing" a possible convert. What's the objection to bringing "influence" to bear if it is the right kind of influence? Certainly there ought not to be unfair pressure, domestic or otherwise, and I do not argue that every other Catholic ought to grab a candle and some holy water and start out to convert the world. There is little danger of that. But why not the influence of a cordial, balanced and kindly attitude? Why not an invitation to try it, to see a parish priest, to think about it anyway? I suppose every priest in America has had the experience of instructing a convert who would have been a Catholic years ago if someone in the family had had the sense to say "come on" in a quiet tone. I suppose also that every rectory parlor in America, to the dismay of the angels, echoes with phrases like these spoken by the converts: "Nobody ever asked me." "I didn't know I could." "I didn't know what to do about it." "I was afraid to come alone." "Well, you see, Dorothy never mentioned it." "I wanted to for years but it just never came up in our house." "I thought if I went to Mass I wouldn't know when to stand up or sit down and I didn't want to ask anybody." Alas. These good, honorable, holy and un-befriended people!

And about that "influence" business again, the series of instructions will take care of that. I mean the parish priest isn't going to grab people with a hook and paste a label on them. He will begin a careful, extended, patient course of lessons, and at the end when the moment of the Declaration of Faith and the Baptism comes, the priest will know the convert as well as any friend in the world.

How long do the instructions last? Usually each appointment runs to a half or three-quarters of an hour. The instructions are once or possibly twice a week, although some priests give more time to each lesson and try to manage more lessons within the week. A lot depends on circumstances. The total course will take about three or four months, more or less, according to progress and individual need. The shortest instruction I ever had was about five minutes, a hospital emergency, and the longest took three years with more sweat and study than I ever did at Our Lady of Angels Seminary. But three or four months is about average.

There is no publicity to the instructions and no publicity about the final Baptism. There is a formal ceremony, but it is private, with two witnesses and the priest, and with only the honored guests who may be invited by the convert. I once knew a man who waited for years because he thought he would be required to stand up before the whole congregation in public display. But then some bold Catholic, some strong, adventurous soul, some radical in our midst, quietly told him it wasn't so. A friend. See what I mean?

MAN OF ALL ARTS

EARLY in the first act of "The Mikado," Ko-Ko, the Lord High Executioner of the Kingdom of Titipu, sings a song about a little list he has compiled of objectionable persons who ought to be executed since "they never will be missed." You may remember it. However, in presenting here a little list of my own, which I put together in an idle moment, I emphatically deny that I am in any manner suggesting that violence be done. I do not argue that there is anything objectionable in the survey to follow; but I certainly do claim that each and every item in it would be missed were it absent.

The list has to do with the priest in your parish. It is not fiction; it is not even theory; the list is simple and everyday fact. Possibly I could, with better grace, leave the catalogue for somebody else to make, but a man outside the priesthood could hardly have access to the secret data involved, so I boldly proceed.

I now offer, for current consideration and for posterity, a partial accounting of the myriad and contrasting roles which any priest, working in a parish, must play in the normal, routine discharge of his duty. Let me declare that all this is not extraordinary. This is pretty common stuff, as your pastor will tell you. I should head the revelations with the title of another song, to wit, "All the Things You Are," except that I believe from listening to the radio that the title implies a certain endearment and I should want to avoid such comment or sentiment here. This is, as I say, pure fact.

To begin with, the parish priest is, or tries to be, a *Spiritual Man*, that is, he must live in his prayers and in his meditations, for otherwise he is useless and he knows it. That's why he goes on a Retreat every year.

Then he is a *Monk* . . . outside of a cloister . . . but a Monk, nevertheless, since he recites the Divine Office every day, gets through the whole of the Psalter every week, and most of the Bible every year.

Then he is a *Priest*, which means that he offers the Sacrifice of the Mass for the living and the dead, administers the sacraments, and uses the powers of Our Lord which came to him at ordination. This would involve care of a Tabernacle, Confessions, Baptism, and Sick Calls. .

Business Man: Actually he manages thousands of dollars and is quite a familiar person in the local bank. He is purchasing agent, investment director, budget manager.

Bookkeeper (Material): Accounts, checkbooks, insurance payrolls and reports.

Bookkeeper (Spiritual): He posts all entries in the death records, the baptismal, first communion and confirmation records, the sick call registry, and the marriage records. With both the Church and the State involved, a single marriage requires four separate and fully detailed sets of entries. We have not mentioned the listing of Mass intentions with dates and names.

Grounds Keeper: He supervises the maintenance of the parish property, i.e., gardens, buildings, lawns, plumbing and heating, roofs, doors, sidewalks, etc., including church, schools, convent and rectory.

Householder: For several people, assistants, etc., he operates a boarding house with meals, general living facilities: keeps good order in the house, if possible.

Collector of Revenue (Internal): He plans the financial program which keeps the parish afloat and persuades people to join in same, supplementing the normal collections with subsidiary supporting events such as parties, bazaars, clubs, and special efforts.

Collector of Revenue (External): Which would be the larger work of charity, education, war relief, missions, hospitals and the full program of the Faith. We do not mention Red Cross, Community Chest, etc.

Diplomat: Which, of course, is a major role and runs through human relations inside and outside the parish, with parishioners and non-parishioners, and through every type of earthly and heavenly crisis.

Theological Student: It is basic that he study, know and apply in a thousand ways and every day, the moral and dogmatic teaching of the Faith.

Teacher: He teaches children their catechism, explaining to minds that range from the third grade to the colleges. He instructs according to the outline of the cycle course on Sundays.

Educational Supervisor: This would be the management of the parish school in the role of Principal, Education Commissioner, Ultimate Disciplinarian, Policy Director and Executive, in cooperation with the Diocesan Office and the faculty of from eight to twenty Sisters. Heavens!

Personal Counselor: This would be the front office of the rectory and everything from family troubles, to financial advice, to alcoholism and the difficulties with in-laws, cooperation with various parole boards and courts, and a broad and profound knowledge of human nature in all its manifestations.

Confessor: This is his sacred and hidden vocation in the formal exercise of the Sacrament of Penance where he is absolutely alone with Christ.

Spiritual Guide: In the manifold direction of souls towards sanctity and in the fostering of vocations.

Lawyer: He applies Canon Law objectively to all decisions in the parish.

Athletics Director: General supervision and promotion of several sports, each in season, with coaches, equipment, discipline, etc.

Playground Superintendent: Which would be all recreational activity not included under the category of athletics.

Census Taker and Director: Which is a very important part of the art of the parish priest for he must know his people by name, address, custom, and family count, state of health and location, including movement and variation in the population. Usually this is both a mental and a card index task.

Preacher: Hoping for spiritual wisdom, doctrinal clarity, rhetorical persuasion, and brevity. Involved here is constant reading, remembering, reference, prudence, and we are bold to state, some thinking.

Missioner: If there are any converts to the Faith, he finds them, instructs them, and receives them into the ancient household. Also if any who are about to fall out of the Faith are saved, he it is who stops them.

Dispatcher: Which is the best word I can find for what would be known in radio as a Program Director and elsewhere as a Starter, i.e., the parish priest prepares the schedule of the Masses, the weddings, the general events of the parish and keeps conflicts of time down to a minimum. This involves consultation of the Ordo and the Seasons of the Faith.

Chaplain: But you could hardly call him a mere chaplain to the Holy Name, the Rosary, the Sodality, the Retreat Group or the Societies, could you? He organizes and keeps them going.

Matrimonial Expert: This, again involves much more than we have space to give, for it would run through the whole complexity from mixed marriages to rehearsals, to arrangements in the far West, to the question of age and general disposition towards responsibility.

Promoter: Communion breakfasts, programs, and all the things which, as the saying is, "have to be worked up."

Literature, Sports, International Politics, etc., which must be followed in order to know what books are good and bad, what movies are decent, and how the Dodgers are doing, and where the communists are loudest.

Chauffeur: For let it be said to end this little list, if not to bring it anywhere near a conclusion, that every last parish priest considers himself to be an expert and an efficient driver, and he has to be.

Not one item in the catalogue is imagined. This is all going on every day in every parish, and I fearlessly write of it here that the general population of the parishes may know what it is they get by way of service from the man who draws a thousand dollars a year, or less, from the parish treasury. Sometimes the roles are split among a couple or several priests; often, very often, the whole panorama is a one-man job. I do not argue that any parish priest is complaining. He loves it. I do not imply that any parish priest thinks that he is put upon or is abused. The priests never stop to count up, and if any of them has the patience to read this, he will be surprised at the length of the list, and will think it rather silly to go to the trouble.

But, now that I have dared thus far, and prescinding, I most sincerely pray, from any personal inclusion, here behind the excuse of a typewriter and the refuge of a desk, I discover I want to pay tribute to the parish priest in this American land. My brothers in black rate a cheer in this or any season, and so be it, here it is.

Do you know what a parish priest is? He is a man who does not believe that there are twenty-four hours in any day. He is a man who once felt the hands of ordination press on his head, and two weeks later looked up to find that he had reached his silver anniversary. He is a man who has more fun than anybody he knows. He is a man who worries more than you think.

Alas, I find I made no mention in the little list of Cemeteries! But as Ko-Ko concludes his song in "The Mikado": "The task of filling up the blanks I'd rather leave to you."

"TO SLEEP, PERCHANCE TO DREAM"

ONCE there was a man whose habit it was to save up thoughts for thinking. He saved them for that time in each day when active work was finished, his prayers all said, and when he was waiting for sleep to claim him. The choice, of course, would be among the happier notions that might occur, the more pleasant themes and the more human and hopeful subjects that might catch at his attention. He was wont to say, "Isn't that interesting? I'll keep that to think about tonight."

You must admit his program has its virtue. Much better than closing the day with worry, or with a mental continuation of what the radio said, or with a summary of threats and fears and discontent. Say your prayers and think a pleasant thought. Not bad.

We now consider the pleasant thought of the gentleman in Chicago who sent five-hundred one-dollar bills through the mail to a list of people picked at random from the telephone book. His letter explained that he was contributing to the Illinois Association for the Crippled, and that he was sending the money "In the belief that every one will come back, and that each dollar will bring several more with it." Now the sequence (which we are to save up till bedtime to ponder) concerns not the man who sent out the money, his ambition, his ingenuity, his skill in making his appeal, but rather we ought to wonder about the people who found the dollar and the letter in the mail. The score read after three weeks by the AP report: 339 replies with additional cash: 72 replies with only the dollar enclosed: 89 who kept what they received and said nothing.

But how did the mind processes work? What did these 500 conclude? (I would ask, "How did they react?" except that that phrase is always reminiscent of chemistry and pills and little apples falling on Newton's head.) How did they construe their obligation? The favorable, extra-cash enclosed replies . . . the 339. Did they say, "Now here's a good guy, I'll help?" Or, "He's a trusting soul, I'll not disillusion him?" Or, "He thinks I won't send his silly dollar back, does he, well, I'll show him." Or, "Maybe there is a pay-off somewhere, I'd better make sure."

Or, "What a grand idea; why didn't somebody do this before? I must tell the Pastor about this . . . the church debt, you know." Or was it, and in how many cases, merely the current submission in the matter of remitting funds by mail to a revenue office?

And the 72 who only sent the dollars back with nothing more? What did they say to themselves? How did they judge the situation? Was it, "This is some swindle, better be safe and stay out." Or, "Miss X, take this gentleman's dollar and send it back to him." Or, "I won't stoop to keeping this dollar, but I pick my own charity, please."

The real fun comes with the 89 who kept the windfall. How did these fell folk explain their actions to themselves? Was it, "Look, here's a guy who thinks he's got a racket, I'll teach him"? Or, "Who does this guy think he is? Ponzi"? Or, "Well of all the nerve!" Or, "Finder's, keepers, brother, so long." Or, "He thinks he can kid me, does he, he and his high pressure stuff!" Or, "Look, Liz, here's some dope who thinks he's Santa Claus . . . on my money, wouldn't ya know?" And how many of the sad 89 are walking around to this day with a reply still in the pocket unmailed, or with a good intention not realized, just waiting to get around to it; and how many thought the letter was advertising and threw it into the basket?

Are you asleep yet? Ever hear of the sheep who couldn't sleep and started counting humans? But just two more sheep, or pleasant thoughts, or dollar bills, or whatever this is about, and we shall have done. It is this. Children have in them the power to make people smile. Notice it some time.

It is very difficult to speak to a child without smiling. Even when you are stern, you are smiling inside. Strangers meeting children on the street go their way thereafter, grinning. Why should this be? We can rule out the grouches who never smile, and the sentimentalists who coo over anything soft, small, and fuzzy. The power remains in the children. They can brighten our eyes, lift our hopes, make optimists of us. Why? Is it because we know innocence is happy? Is this a tribute we pay to sinlessness? Is it because children are a promise that the world will have another chance? Are we drawn here to give of our best, and therefore we smile? Is it that a child is a triumph, an achievement in a worried world, and we are glad because if the child is a hope not yet fulfilled, he is not a hope that has been lost, or soiled, or discouraged?

G. K. Chesterton wrote somewhere that since Bethlehem and the first sight of the Mother and the Child, a reflection of Their grace, a part of Their unearthly light, a portion of the power and the lure and the attraction towards good which They have, rests upon any mother with any child in her arms. He was writing of a profound truth of the Faith, the truth that takes all things to itself.

One last thought: it could be a good bet that no Catholic ever watched any production of Shakespeare without assuming that all the characters were Catholic also. It is almost inevitable. You can hardly miss the atmosphere, and you feel at home in the language. Above all, you recognize the thoughts and the issues in the plays. We wager here, of course, in no sense of boasting about Shakespeare, in no narrow spirit and with knowledge that Shakespeare lived in the age of Elizabeth when the Church was persecuted in England.

There is some scholarly discussion as to whether Shakespeare himself was faithful to the old religion. Some say he didn't live, but died, a Catholic. But whatever his habits of a Sunday, the man certainly wrote and taught as a Catholic, and the plays give incontrovertible testimony. The momentum, the gorgeous drive and lunge of the action and the imagery come of the old tradition of the Faith—Free Will, Conscience, Responsibility, Sin, Temptation, Life after Death—and without these things there would be no Shakespeare plays. They are the stuff his dreams are made on.

To speak but a moment more of Hamlet. In the very first scene when the Ghost appears, Horatio, wishing to test the specter says: "I'll cross it though it blast me." Actors then make a sign of the cross. Of course. The script demands it since the full speech is this: "I'll cross it though it blast me. . . . Stay illusion! If thou hast any sound or use of voice, speak to me: if there be any good thing to be done that may do thee ease, and grace to me, speak to me." But that is the Catholic doctrine of the living man offering succor to a dead man and thereby gaining grace. This is, simply, the impulse of All Souls' Day.

In the scene with Ophelia at her prayers. a prie-dieu is usually set against the wall. The little half-chapel often has a blue triptych and the image is the figure of Our Lady. How natural. How right it seems for the prayers of the young girl.

And the language of Hamlet! "What is a man, if his chief good and market of his time be but to sleep and feed? A beast, no more. Sure, He that made us with such large discourse, looking before and after, gave us not that capability and godlike reason to fust in us unused." Sounds like a sermon on a retreat.

Again, the scene where Hamlet is tempted to kill the King, but while the King is at prayer: "Now might I do it pat, now while he is praying; and now I'll do it. . . . And so he goes to heaven; and so am I revenged. That would be scann'd: a villain kills my father; and for that, I his sole son, do this same villain send to heaven. . . . No!"

The quotations could be multiplied. They do ring out in the theatre like phrases of home, and church, and altar. But—Thought: it's time to stop. Thought No. 2: I will. Goodnight.

CONFESSIONS AT SEVEN-THIRTY

Not as the shuffling line of men
That crawls in the street and meanly sups
On bread that bears a crust of scorn
And bitterness stirred in steaming cups:
Nor as the file of tittering children
Ranked by sizes and made to walk
By watching eyes to rooms that smell
Of books and varnish and dust of chalk:
And not as those expectant ones
Who crowd a red gold foyer to wait
Their hour of floating beyond themselves
To shadowed places and gayer fate:
O not as these they stand, but as a row
Dark Lucifer might see
And with his broken angels
Look on enviously.

Shadows almost hide them as they go,
Slowly at the sound of sliding doors,
And one, by one, by one, in patient row
They step behind some curtains in the wall,
Where seated there is one who stoops to hear
Old words that tell a story old as flesh.
Impersonally . . . a disembodied ear . . .
He sighs, then gestures with a power
Strange as Mercy was at Calvary's hour.

Once long ago the Writer in the sand
Had said: "*Whose sins you shall forgive . . .*"
So one by one by one in rows they stand.
Faint rattle of beads: quick smothered coughs;
Soft sound of lips at prayer . . . and then . . .
Swish of clothing: scuffle of a shoe:
The door slides gratingly again.

Who stands there? All the world,
But only God may know
And him whose secret heart
Is as a scripture furled.

Innocence untried with lisping voice,
Dim-eyed innocence with graying hair,
Maybe Judas stands beside a little child,
Who knows? The varied world is waiting there.
Fighters, surrenderers, Johns and Magdalens,
Bringing sorrow, hearts in sackcloth, scarred,
Lame with lust, halt with sin, blind,
Pharisee and saint and dicing guard!
"Whose sins you shall forgive . . ."
O not as men who beg the streets for bread.
What good is bread? Did Dismas ask for it?
Was that Augustine's hunger? David's want?
For bread were Pentecostal fires lit?
The door slides again and so they go
At seven-thirty standing in a row.
Shrill whistles come from outside, and the bleat
Of horns is restless in the moving street.
One, by one, by one . . .
Dark Lucifer might see
And look on, enviously.

Of something drifting through delighted air.

NEW LIGHT IN THE SKY

I T IS all beginning again. The fresh, young wonder of discovery is starting to happen. I mean Springtime, the magic moment when you find that the days are getting longer, and that at six o'clock the light is still in the sky. The ice is porous, two inches off the edge of the road, with triumphant water running under it. The cement walk is dry, actually dry, and not merely bare. There are other signs: the undetermined and half-defeated appearance of a snow squall; the sudden brightness of the sun through a window, if even only briefly; the sound of people walking without rubbers; the delight of a temperature in the fifties; the car starting at the first push on the gadget. These mean Spring with all the spirit's high delight at puddles and a patch of sky. It's beginning to happen again.

But I mean more than that, for to the Catholic the Springtime brings Lent; the season of the weather is intertwined with the season of the soul, and the new discovery of familiar, old and very dear signs is happening now in his Faith. Spring is beginning, but Lent is beginning too, and the youthful, buoyant happiness is much the same.

One Sunday the priest reads the Lenten Regulations, and the cadence of them falls from the pulpit like a song long remembered, half forgotten, and now heard again. "With the exception of Sundays, all the days of Lent are fast days of obligation. The Lenten fast and abstinence end at noon on Holy Saturday." We could guess that most people in the pews could recite it by heart. "All persons between the ages of twenty-one and fifty-nine are obliged to fast except: women in delicate health and condition: the sick and convalescent: those engaged in hard labor or duties

57

of an exhaustive nature . . ." The very words and phrases, like
the blue skies, like the warmer sun, haven't changed in the memory of man. They are ancient, they are ever new. It's Lent again.
"Custom allows the use of some warm drink in the morning such
as tea, coffee or cocoa, with a piece of bread." It's Lent again.
Catholic life is returning to sweet and familiar places. And if you
are very attentive, you even recognize the little shock of the
mind at the implication that there are some apparently, who take
cocoa for breakfast!

"The law of abstinence forbids the eating of meat and soups
made of meat." We do not, certainly, mean to be irreverent, but
does not the sentence fall on the ear like the sound of the first
Spring robin? It is like a signal to begin a new part of life. It
does, I think, once a year, what the sentence, "The prayers of
the congregation are requested this morning . . ." does every
Sunday for the Catholic. It tells that the Faith is going on, is
alive.

Then a Wednesday is Ash Wednesday and brings again the
somber mark made on the forehead with the words: "Remember
man that thou art dust and unto dust thou shalt return." People
do understand the sobriety of this symbol. How could they miss
its significance? They are prayerful, intent, recollected. This is a
serious moment. This really means the penitential season. But
what we should notice in this context is the contentment and
the lift in the ceremony. People are eager to come forward to
be touched with the ash. There is a confidence, a pleasantness, a
return to familiar things in Ash Wednesday that perhaps is in-
expressible except that you have been doing this since childhood
when you gloried in a particularly dark and emphatic smudge.

It is rather like hearing the gospel about the mustard seed and
finding it both old and new; like remembering to go to Mass on
that holy day that comes in the midst of August heat; or even
like not being surprised at how many coal collections there always

seem to be. Only, of course, Ash Wednesday means Lent and the Springtime.

The churches will be lighted now for two extra evenings in the week. After supper families will get ready for the "devotions." The preaching will be regular and strenuous on the Tuesday or Wednesday nights. Father So and So from St. X's parish will be recommended with as much regard for actual fact as is possible, and the congregation will be urged to attend in numbers "during this holy season." It's all beginning again: the definite, the distinctive experience of being Catholic is returning to a familiar phase.

On Fridays there are the Stations of the Cross with the surpliced priest, the candles, the tall crucifix, the line of altar boys proceeding up the aisles, and the voice of the priest sounding through the church from unusual places. "The Fourth Station: Jesus Meets His Afflicted Mother." "We adore Thee, O Christ, and we bless Thee." And then the murmured response of the congregation: "Because by Thy holy Cross Thou hast redeemed the world." They genuflect; they stand, turn in the direction of the priest to look upon the Station that portrays the holy event in the world's salvation. At intervals, the sad, reverent, unforgettable melody of the Stabat Mater sobs to Heaven as the priest and the boys, the candles and the tall crucifix move on toward the next Station.

It is the Springtime part, the Lenten part of being Catholic. Some hopeful, eternally young and undefeated inner response of the soul is here. We are glad that this has come again, and looking ahead, even in the very beginning of the season, we are conscious of what awaits us at the end in the great climax of the Holy Week.

These days are not merely times of penance, of fasting, of additional abstinence. This is not merely a season when we all decide to discipline ourselves. There is an anticipation in these weeks, a sense of waiting, a feeling of promise and a progress toward a magnificent fulfillment. That's what makes Lent for us:

it leads somewhere. A triumph, a victory, a tremendous, crashing drama lie at the end of it. Already we feel its power. We do not fast just for the sake of fasting. All this heightened and more intense life of the Church does not proceed in a vacuum. We know what's ahead of us. We are moving toward a crisis and the day will come when the Church will cry: *"Hosannah to the Son of David: blessed is He who cometh in the name of the Lord,"* and we will hold palm branches and stand again at the moment when all time and eternity come to a focus. It is Springtime again in the Faith.

We shall see again the whiteness, the hush, the ineffable calm of a Holy Thursday when the bells ring and then are silent as the movement of Redemption turns to the unveiled cross of the Good Friday. The church will be empty, the Tabernacle door swung wide, the linens stripped, the lamps put out. Then early in the dawn, the priest, like an everlasting prophet, will move with fire in his hands from the church porch to the interior, to the gates of the sanctuary. The lamps will be relighted from the fire. The long telling of God's plans will be recited in the twelve Old Testament prophecies. Slowly, deliberately after the blessing of water and a Baptismal font, after a twice repeated Litany, in measured certainty, the priest of Christ will approach the altar for the long delayed moment of utter bliss. *"Gloria in excelsis,"* he will sing, and all the earth must hear him.

The bells ring out "Alleluia!" and the Church which seemed dead comes alive. It is the Day of the Resurrection, and all the delighted air, the new lift and surge in life, the young infectious gladness of Spring will be justified and made real.

It is all beginning again, and a new light is in our sky.

FORMULA FOR RAIN

FOR reasons that, I am sure, will be painfully obvious to all in any drenched Spring, a line out of Stephen Benét's minor poems keeps coming to mind. The title is "Nightmare," and the poem begins:

> It rained quite a lot that Spring. You woke in the morning
> And saw the sky still clouded, the streets still wet,
> But nobody noticed much, except the taxis
> And the people who parade.
> You don't in a city.
> The parks got very green . . .

It keeps coming back, and back again . . . "It rained quite a lot that Spring . . ."

You have noticed the rains. Everybody has who yearns for the ball park, the golf meadows, or a dry hour to hang out the clothes. Have you not noticed that, getting out to Mass these May mornings, and coming home these May evenings? If *everybody* in the world had commonly planned for a huge picnic, it couldn't rain more. It has been raining for weeks.

Now this can cause a certain mildewed condition in the human spirit, a droop in the inner courage, a damp and soggy lump in the area of the soul, and we, perhaps, should mutually consult about what we are to do about it.

One of the wise observations of Catholic theology is that the weather can have something to do with your prayers, and even with your temptations, but that it doesn't matter much because moods don't count. It is easy to feel holy in the sunshine, and just as easy to feel gloomy about salvation in the rain. The Church says feelings don't count, and the Church is right. After being assured of that, should we not try to assist each other even on the spiritually insignificant level of emotions?

Let me confess I have no infallible defense against rains. Sometimes it helps to think of all the little onions growing in the ground. They must be very happy about the wet. Sometimes it bolsters the mind to try to remember the ancient appearance of sunshine, or what dust was. Words like Sahara, or feathers, or sandpaper, can be useful, if repeated verbally with the shades down. It is dehydrating too to remember that the saints speak of something they call dry rot in the soul. Dry, mind you.

None of these may be of any value to you, and ought not to be urged against your own inclinations. You may be a What-Can-I-Do-About-It man, or a So-What person, although these attitudes towards anything are not characteristically Catholic. You may be a fatalist, and that is certainly not Catholic, but I doubt that we have many fatalists among readers of this book . . . ascetic, penitential folks, surely, but not fatalists.

So I do not insist on these lesser methods, but proceed to more vigorous defenses against rain which ought to be seized upon. They are sovereign in power.

Turn on all the lights in the house. If in an office, turn on all the lights in the office, or the shop, or the market. Wherever you are, turn on all the lights. You will be amazed at the result. Lights are often considered to be mere illumination, and turned on only for the purpose of sight, but this is a narrow and meager fallacy. Light is a happy thing. God made light as a gift in which to be gay and buoyant. Turn them on when it rains and make a party of it.

Don't ever, don't ever read novels during these trying times. Especially don't read any novel written since the days of William Makepeace Thackeray. Novels are filled with frustrated, anguished, and agonizing people who will depress you more and more. There are few stories in any modern novel. A good story would be ashamed to get into a modern novel. Modern novels are full of groanings which pass for conversation, full of ephemera that pass for thought, full of blasphemy that substitutes for reality. Have nothing to do with novels on a rainy day.

Read, rather, on a dreary day such poetry as can spin pin-wheels in your head. There *is* poetry of this kind, superior to any weather. A good rousing speech out of Shakespeare can do it. Better still, something specifically spun on the glories of the

Faith. Gerard Manley Hopkins is filled with such, and each one is so profound and brilliant that the mind is reluctant to let go. For instance, there are the lines on "The Blessed Virgin Compared to the Air We Breathe." Fine title for May. Here is a small part: "I say that we are wound with mercy round and round as if with air; the same is Mary, more by name. She, wild web, wondrous robe, mantles the guilty globe, since God has let dispense her prayers His providence: nay, more than almoner, the sweet alms' self is her, and men are meant to share her life as life does air. . . . If I have understood, she holds high motherhood towards all our ghostly good and plays in grace her part about man's beating heart, laying, like air's fine flood the death dance in his blood. . . ."

If you still feel depressed about incessant rains, and the general gloom, go find a child and look long and meekly at his face. Any child will do if the age is between seven and ten. You have to be serious about it, and speak simple, unpatronizing words. You have to mean it when you say the grass is green, or the wind is laughing. If you are serious and make it clear you do mean everything honestly, you will suddenly feel the miracle. Everything is wonderful, and new, and fresh, and marvelous, at seven to ten. Even rains are wonderful when they rinse every day. The gift and the magic gaiety of God are plain. It helps when you are tired to see the face of a child.

Now that we have come here to a merciful end, and are full of hope that the rain, like this essay, must cease, let me offer two more secrets to use during difficult hours. Never let a decision be made before breakfast and a cup of coffee. Resolutely follow through what you decided the night before.

Pay no attention to what you think at three o'clock in the morning of a sleepless night. The world is a dull, dark, and catastrophic place at three o'clock on a sleepless night, and you seem the worst catastrophe in it. Pay no attention. You will look more possible by noon.

SPIRITUAL ARITHMETIC

AT THOSE moments when we begin to think that we are doing a great deal for God in giving of actual time to His worship, then the method of spiritual arithmetic may possibly come to our rescue. Statistics can be compiled. Figures can be added up. We can discover the exact portion of our time given formally to the Creator.

Let us begin with the matter of attendance at the Holy Mass. Surely nothing is more basic to the Catholic life, nothing is more common. We sometimes boast, and our friends outside the Faith sometimes remark: "There is one thing about the Catholics . . . they do go to Mass on Sunday." Well, how does it add up in a busy and active life?

For the total, normal Mass-life, the figure of 60 years is a fair and typical average. Few begin to go to Mass, at least with any attention or knowledge, before the age of 7. Sixty years of worship from that age would bring the faithful Catholic soul to the maturity of 67 years. Now, I am well aware that many souls keep going to Mass, loyally and well, into the 70's and even into the 80's. May the Lord bless them and give them peace. But on the other hand, many are not able to continue at Mass through all the 60 years. Life ends, illness comes, negligence rots, a thousand hindrances may intrude, so that the figure of a full 60 years is a generous and copious average.

Now, there are 52 Sundays in every year, and 6 Holy Days of Obligation. Presuming a perfect attendance, with no absences, that would make 58 times a year that the Catholic soul offers to God the repeating Sacrifice of Calvary. But to make the arithmetic easier, and to give us what are called round numbers, let us throw in one funeral and one wedding to make the total 60 for any year. Please remember that we are thinking here of perfect attendance. Please remember that we are thinking of the ideal year when neither the weather, nor disposition, nor misfortune get in the way. A perfect year would mean 60 Masses offered.

The next step is simple: 60 Masses for each of 60 years would mean that in a full lifetime the Catholic soul would attend Mass 3,600 times. At first glance that would seem to be a large number, a reason for some complacence, a brave and worthy total.

But let us say that each Mass takes a full half hour of time, or 30 minutes. Again that estimate is fair and general because it presumes that the Catholic is never late, never comes in "before the Book is changed," and therefore feels safe, and never leaves during the recitation of the Last Gospel of St. John telling about the *"Light shining in the darkness but the darkness did not comprehend."* A half hour is, indeed, a fair estimate. So, 30 minutes of time expended in 3,600 Masses brings us to a grand total of 108,000 minutes. Heavens! We are reaching into six-digit figures! 108,000 does look substantial and solid. Alas, however, we are dealing in minutes only.

There are 60 minutes in an hour. 108,000 minutes comes out to 1,400 hours which is a little less impressive. Remember that all this is the total lifetime contribution, the complete story. There are 24 hours in each day, and 24 as we used to say in school, goes into 1,400 something slightly over 58 times. The figure is 58 and a fraction; but again for the sake of ease, let us be very generous and say the result is 59. Therefore in a whole lifetime, a faithful, perfect, untardy Catholic soul would give 59 days to Mass.

There are 30 days in some months, 31 days in others. The full and final figure is that the soul gives to God either 1 or 2 days less than 2 months in a full and scrupulous lifetime of Mass attendance! Yes, that is the figure: less than 2 months.

By comparison, a man spends much more than that going to and from his work, much more than that in sleeping, more than that eating, than that listening to the radio. I once saw a figure to indicate that a man spends in excess of three months in his life in the process of shaving! We shall in charity and in ignorance, omit any reference to the ladies' mystic rites of, their preoccupation with, a lipstick. How much time does all that take?

As I have said, at those moments when we begin to think that we are doing a great deal for God in the giving of actual time to His worship, the spiritual arithmetic helps. After a whole life-time, we offer to the Most High a grand total sum of something less than two months.

HIS OWN GREAT FRIENDS

To LIVE within the Faith is to be related, to be in association with Persons. There are times and moods when Catholicism seems to be essentially that. Christmastime would be one of them for we then look up and find ourselves belonging to a group that has in it the Child, the Mother, and St. Joseph.

Any Communion time would be another, for then we are actually in union with a Person. Receiving the Most Blessed Sacrament means being joined with Christ. It is a tremendous thing, but it is also a very simple, a very human thing. We are united with Him.

A brief visit to a Church would be another of these for we genuflect to recognize that He is there; we kneel to consider Whom we are with; the whole purpose in a visit is not so much to formally pray, which can be done anywhere, but to speak to Him Who is here . . . with us and near us now. So much of being a Catholic is the holding of a bond with Our Lord.

And this month of May is another period when the personal relationship within the Faith is very obvious because this month we especially feel we belong to Our Lady, and she belongs to us. It's as easy as that and as normal as that with the Catholic. She is Christ's Mother, and through her relation to Him and our relation to Him, we are brought into a most warm, and welcome, and happy, and hopeful, and glad association with her.

In a sense we are all friends who know each other, and the

magnificence of it, the awesome privilege, cannot make less true
the essential simplicity. The Faith is people belonging to each
other, and if some of the people are People, it only indicates
the privilege and the grace. It does not destroy the glorious fact
of the bond.

The little catechism declares this when it defines the Church:
"The congregation of all those who profess the Faith of Christ"
. . . . We are apt to get into formalities by that word "congregation," and think of pews with faces ranged in them, of a religious
corporation, of a society in the meaning of an organized group.
That is included in the meaning of the term, but "congregation"
also means people who are simply gathered together, who hold
a kinship among themselves.

First and causing all the others is the bond with Christ. Next
and highest after Our Lord is the beautiful belonging to Our
Lady. Then come the Saints, of course. There are St. Francis, St.
Vincent, St. Peter, St. Paul, St. Teresa, St. Bernadette and all
the good company of whom you are allowed to have your
favorites, your special friends. We are all associated with one
another: the Church is "the congregation of all those who profess
the Faith of Christ . . ." It is a meeting of ourselves.

The notion goes even beyond what we have suggested, and
that is why there is no such thing as a Catholic who is completely
strange to any other Catholic. In being related to Our Lord we
are already introduced to each other. This is what Paul meant by
the Mystical Body of Christ, but approached from the idea of a
human association, of a wide, varied company of people who hold
ties among themselves, the dogma becomes vivid and human and
immensely enriching.

Within the Church we do hold the same bundle of doctrine;
we do live by the same code, we do become holy in the same
Sacraments, but in addition we all belong to a companionship
that is very real and very good. Nationality does not matter, race
does not matter, condition of life does not alienate. There are no

boundary lines on the earth or in time, for the association breaks through time and death and physical disappearance, and it holds everywhere, and always.

The ideal of durability is mentioned, and hoped for, and intended, in all good bonds among human beings. We say: "I shall always be your friend." We say: "You can always count on me." Or, "I am your friend and I shall never fail you." It's the *always* that is the ideal, the pledge and the test. The notion of *forever* is forever in what we want in our loves.

The splendor of the Faith is precisely here: Our Lord is always there, Our Lady is always our own, the bonds with the Saints, with fellow Catholics are always our own, the same, and will endure forever. God did manifest His Love for us in the concept and in the establishment of His Faith on the earth, but His love took into account what we are and what we need. The Faith is not an outside thing imposed on men: it meets the needs of men as they are, and it fits our inside nature.

"It is not good for man to be alone," said the Creator. In the Faith He has given His Son, His Son's Mother, His Own great friends, and all of us together, that we be not alone.

ON, AND ON, AND ON

It is really quite proper and quite dignified to say that Easter is a festival of the Faith which bursts upon our altars. The great day does not merely arrive, like a date on a calendar; it explodes like an Event which the Faith has been keeping for a surprise.

In Easter something definitely has been touched off. There is a blast in this day; there is an uproar here, a vehemence, and even a violence. Easter does not come; it bursts. People who had been coming to Mass each Sunday come again on this Sunday and discover that the altar is shooting with lilies, fountained with flowers, that the organ is pulsing in great chords, that the flame of a Pascal candle is waving and burning, and that the music surges into a shouting: "Alleluia! Alleluia!"

Of course those fortunate souls who have been following the Faith through the whole of Holy Week understand this bursting best. It comes out so suddenly on Holy Saturday morning after the silence and the somber movements of Good Friday. The ceremonies of Holy Saturday proceed quietly and intently. Then a moment arrives after the long Litanies. The bells ring, the organ thunders, and the first Alleluia rides out like the cry of a trumpet. It is Easter in the Faith.

But even those who do not follow the complete and dynamic drama can catch the excitement of it on the Sunday. *"He is risen, He is not here: behold the place where they laid Him!"* Doubtless that is why the crowds of Easter all leave the sanctuaries with smiles on their faces. Nobody can be spiritually calm on the day of the Resurrection.

With all this in our experience, may I be forgiven if I indulge in a private notion of my own which amounts to an inner compulsion at Easter? It is a happy notion and seems most valid in the sunshine around an Empty Tomb.

To begin, let us remember that we Catholics are a very old people in the world. We have a lot of history behind us. We are, indeed, the ancient Church. Our teachers and orators and our preachers are forever reminding us of the long, long past. And it is a good thing too, because the Church is the oldest living society on earth. The Church is unique, unmatched, unrivaled, singular in human history. There is nothing like the Church anywhere on the scene.

The coins in the museum show the face of Caesar Augustus. The Church remembers him as the Church remembers Charlemagne, and Nero, and Napoleon, and Attila, and Constantine. Our vestments are the garments of the Roman street. Our language is the speech of the Roman senate.

We sailed with Columbus, and we saw the rise of Europe out of the primitive forests. We are older than France, and we recall the time when a Pope sent missioners to civilize England. The Goths and the Vandals are folk we tamed and taught to shave; and Greeks and Ethiopians were our first bishops and heroes. Why, we once read the letters of St. Paul in a familiarity as easy as next Sunday's announcements.

We are ancient and we are unchanged, and, as I say, it is a fine thing to keep this all in mind.

But there can be a too exclusive concentration on the ancient. There can be too much preoccupation with the past. Catholics are people with a future. The signs of life are on us. The direction is forward, and we belong not only to the closed records of the past, but also to the adventure of the time that is to come. Our Lord is a risen Lord, and our Feast is an explosion. The Faith is a society that endures, lasts, lives, and wins.

Nobody can tell what trials and what anguish lie ahead for the Faith, but can we indulge ourselves at Easter to think that the time will come when the Catholics of the Twenty-second Century or the Catholics of the Thirty-second Century will look back on Pius XII challenging the Communists much as we now look back on the Pontiff who challenged Attila and the Huns? They will then think of the annoyances that accompanied the beginning of the Atomic Age as we think of the troubles that fretted the early Middle Ages. They will recall the missions to the Orient as we remember the Jesuits who came to the forests of the Mohawk, and speak of the present Cardinal of China as we speak of John Carroll of the See of Baltimore.

The future is with the risen Lord, and we must never conclude that a place, called Europe, was ever big enough to encompass Catholicism. Hilaire Belloc has a phrase in which he says: "Europe is the Faith," and with that we can thoroughly agree; but he finishes his phrase by saying that, "the Faith is Europe," and with that I most humbly and respectfully debate to the point of rejection. If Europe has lost the Faith, then it's just too bad for Europe. It may be fair France, or merry England, or sunny Italy that is gone, but they are only nations that once had a chance. The Faith is no more limited to Europe than it was limited to North Africa when North Africa had Augustine to teach it.

The day will come when the Faith will remember the Reformation as a youthful rebellion of boys in the early experience of Catholicism in the world; and scholars will study the sects as they now study the vagaries of the Semi-Pelagians, and the Cathari, and the Arians. The Communists will come to look very much like the wild Goths and the Vandals. We then, we Catholics of Post-World-War-II will be numbered as the early Fathers of Christianity when we shall have joined with the bones of the Faithful buried in the catacombs.

Never should we be so complacent that we avoid the need to struggle, and be holy, and to recognize a profound crisis in the Faith when it faces us. We can be certain of the future because it does not depend on us; but we can never presume on the future because the only way to the future is through the present, and the present is our responsibility. There will be much darkness and suffering and confusion yet. But we do fight on a winning side.

Such, then, is the private and happy notion engendered and made articulate by all the Alleluias ringing through the Easter air.

There is one sad place that we ought also to keep seeing through the lilting ceremonies of Holy Saturday, and the bursting of the Easter Masses. It is that red tomb of Lenin in Moscow. That's where they keep the founder of communism in Russia. He is embalmed there, and is exhibited to the long lines of people who come silently in, to pass by the glass-covered coffin. He has been there since 1920. Ice water circulates through his veins; this corpse pulses with formaldehyde blood; it blushes in rouge; it is stiffened in a vacuum. And there it is: Lenin in his dead, red tomb.

He is a challenge, Lenin. Communism is reaching out and the doctrine of the dead is spreading. The horror, the cold contagion, the clammy conquest of the corpse is sinking over the land. We may suffer much and wrestle much against this adversary with the chemical bloods. But let us be of good courage, and let us be in good confidence.

The Tomb we stand by is empty. The place round which we rally is a broken grave. The challenge is against Him Who *"led captivity captive."*

Listen! Can you not hear? *"Put in thy finger hither, and see my hands, and bring hither thy hand and put it into my side. . . ."*

Easter is a day for the future. The vision here is outward . . . and on, and on, and on.

CATHOLICS OF ALL SIZES

THERE is a very definite sense of spiritual relaxation that follows Easter. It is as though great issues had been in contention and now had been settled in our favor; as though great risks and great turmoil had been passed and we had now achieved a calm and a peace. The feeling, of course, is the return to a normal living in the Faith, the usual, calm Providence of God, the ordinary chances at Divine grace which the Death and the Resurrection of Christ made to be our daily opportunity. After Easter the Church sails on the level seas of time.

In a mood of ease and retrospect, therefore, we might recall two or three very minor stories suited to this season of calm. The first has to do with the weather of Holy Thursday. The sun shone on Holy Thursday, and it shone promptly and decisively at sunrise. Holy Thursday ceremonies and the Mass are scheduled early in the parishes, and not much past 6:30 A.M. there they were, this group of scrubbed, buoyant altar boys, twittering in the sunlight outside the side door of the church. Surplices were starched and white. The bright morning sun was like sudden triumph as you met it.

The boys were excited because high in a tree, single, alone, perfectly visible was a fat red robin. They were eager to point him out. Against the clear blue of the sky, the robin was a patch of gay color. The white surplices, the washed blue of the sky, the fine etching of the tree, the burnished breast of the robin, the abundant sun were a subject for a painter's brush.

"Maybe he knows it's Holy Thursday," ventured one of the boys. "Naw," said another, "you have to be people to know it's Holy Thursday." He went on, this philosopher of the group, to say in addition, "You have to be people to know anything." The larger issue was not taken up. The boys seemed content with the immediate privilege of being people and knowing at this bright morning moment that it was Holy Thursday.

We must also report that the Holy Saturday ceremonies for the blessing of Baptismal water contain a great power over the mind. The ceremonies are very rich and impressive, and they involve the holding of a great Paschal candle by one of the boys, and then the placing of the candle in the water being blessed for use in the Sacrament. The young man holding the candle, standing in the circle around the font with the other young men, was afflicted with a case of hiccoughs. The hiccough can be devastating when it comes out of the silence. Well, I have to report that such is the interest and the power of the Holy Saturday ritual that not one giggle followed even after the fourth hiccough. The young men were absorbed in the candle, the holy oils, the water, the long and lovely processes of Holy Saturday. The hiccoughs meant nothing.

You will have to supply your own interpretation and comment on this next minor episode. It concerns Sisters, and I dare not, beyond the simple statement of fact. The boys, this time, were violently discussing the truth that there are several kinds of Sisters. Some teach, "like our Sisters," one boy declared. "Some are nurses," said another. Now this last contribution to the forum had a deeper knowledge that included cloisters and the vocations of prayer. In a spirit of pure science and with conscious knowledge he offered the information: "There's other Sisters too; some are clustered and some are semi-clustered."

And last, let us look at another Holy Thursday event, for it could happen anywhere. The three very juvenile pilgrims had met outside the main door of the church. They were ambitious to enter, for this was Holy Thursday, and in height they ranged from small to smaller to smallest. The small and the smaller were attempting to prevent the entrance of the smallest. He didn't prevent easily. He protested. He would assert his rights and he did. He shouted to the other two a final retort: "This church is for Catholics of all sizes!"

"This church is for Catholics of all sizes," he had said, and he came very close to speaking a summary of many of Our Lord's parables about the nature of the Church. Our Lord called the Church a net into which all sorts of fish came. Our Lord called the Church a mustard tree to which all kinds of birds flew. And here on Holy Thursday the young man was arguing, "This church is for Catholics of all sizes." Good for him. He's right. He's absolutely right. Indeed, he is profound if you ponder a moment on what he said.

SIGHTS, SOUNDS, AND WEATHER

THE thesis about to be developed here, obviously, is not profound, but I am hopefully sure that much of it will be familiar. It is this: there are Catholic sights and Catholic sounds, and there is even such a thing as Catholic weather. Certain sights and sounds, and certain variations in the weather, in our experience with Catholicism, have come to mean the Faith, and we have made of them, perhaps unconsciously, a whole series of unintended sacramentals.

Children walking slowly in a line with white veils on their heads are instantly recognized as Catholic. While caps and berets have become popular substitutes at Confirmation time, there are those of us who still prefer the veils as against the newer trends, on the basis of the instant identification. White veils on the heads of little girls make a Catholic sight for the heart to behold.

Another sight would be a crowd of people hurrying up the street in the early hours of a Sunday: another would be a lady with a purse tucked under her arm but with a big, black Missal held in her hand. A man pausing on the church steps to brush his trousers at the knees may be observed in any neighborhood. A line of automobiles stretched along the curb at 5:30 in the morning is a Catholic sight indicating a holy day. If you see a double file of children turning a corner, you may know that two Sisters are walking at the head, and if you wait long enough, two more Sisters will swing around the corner at the end of the ranks.

This is not strictly true, and perhaps we should not mention it, but there are people who feel that there is something distinctly Catholic about a fish market. They confess to a frequent sense of fraternity to other customers in the place, as if—and this cannot always be true—they were all Catholic together and bent on errands of abstinence. Some Catholics do not like fish, but we may suppose that these conceive a similar implication on the sight of an egg.

Again, a young girl moving out to the street with a handkerchief over her hair indicates that she has made a Visit, and has found a way to obey St. Paul even though she has forgotten her hat. Lighted candles, everywhere, even on a dinner table suggest the Faith to a Catholic; and charcoal is a definitely Catholic substance to a Catholic boy. A funeral procession before noon argues that the procession is coming from a Requiem Mass. A man sitting ahead in the bus may not be a priest, but if he is wearing a black hat, you look twice to be sure, and if, in addition, he is wearing a black coat you instinctively search for a Roman Collar.

As corollary to the general thesis, let us digress to remark that there are also Catholic numbers, and among them, the numbers 3, 7 and 40 are the most conspicuous. Three means the Trinity, the hours of our Redemption, Faith, Hope and Charity, the total of the Wise Men and the total within the Holy Family. Seven means the seven Sacraments and the seven Capital Sins. Forty is Lent.

After the sights, there are recognizable sounds which are Catholic in what they mean and, indeed, the catalogue of them would be longer than the sights. For a priest standing at the altar for a Mass, the sound of people rising to their feet behind his back is a Catholic sound, and means that the moment of the Gospel is noticed. The noise of steps in the aisles indicates the late-comers are arriving. A kind of sudden and intense sibilance be-hind the priest at Mass means that the boy on the left has called the attention of the boy on the right to his omission in the matter of moving the book.

Such sounds may be special to the priesthood, but any Catholic would recognize the sound of the slide grating as it is opened or closed in the confessional. It echoes through the silent church and means that the line advances by one more, and that an un-burdening of conscience has ended, and that another is about to begin. It is a sound like nothing else in the world, and there is peace within it, and ease, and confidence, for this is the sound of Saturdays, of Christmas Eve, the sound that Our Lord implicitly inaugurated when He said: *"Whose sins you shall forgive, they are forgiven. . . ."*

Did you ever listen to the sound of the Rosary being recited in public, that is, listen to the sound as sound? It is like a wave breaking on a beach, like a tide beating on a shore. First comes the single voice of the priest, and then in answer, the full, falling response: "Holy Mary, Mother of God . . ." Then the priest again, and once more the wave of the answering congregation. It is like a surf, the pouring of a flood and a sea, bearing in crescendo the praise of Gabriel till the end of time, fulfillment of Our Lady's prophecy in the Magnificat, and the sound of petition, and need, and love, rising before the attentive Mother of Christ.

Quickly to get on, the knock of beads that swing and strike against a pew; the slam of a kneeler as it is put down too abruptly; the cough and the rustle of a priest within the confessional; the swish of Sisters as they pass in the aisle; the low pronouncing of the Latin, and especially the repeated prayer spoken over each soul at the Communion rail, and the awesome advance of that murmured sound as the priest comes near . . . all these are Catholic, and they stir inevitable response in the Catholic heart.

We could continue with the chime of a bell rung three times in succession, the chant of the liturgy, the unforgettable melody of the Preface which cannot lose its power even when we hear it over the radio in a chance discovery of a broadcast Mass; the rhythm of the sonorous Latin at a Forty Hours, at a funeral, or on a Holy Saturday . . . these, too, are Catholic sounds, but they are closer to being real sacramentals than the others, for they have been directed by the Church, and are an essential part of our ceremonial. They do mean the Faith; they are recognizable in Catholic living; and they are signs of what Wisdom has been at work to make them so familiar and so dear.

There is another Catholic sound, but it may be more of an accent, or an emphasis, and it may be that it differs in sections of the Catholic world, and even from parish to parish. I mean the stresses and the beat within the words of a recited prayer. Children in a parochial school, for instance, when heard through a window opened to the Spring, sound like this: *"Hourr Fa*ther Who *art* in *Heav*en . . ."* I will contend that the spacing and the fall of the accent in the childish trebles are holy and Catholic music. *"Bless* us, O Lord, and *these* Thy *gifts*. . . ."*

Small matters? But the living of the Faith is made up of small matters: like looking up at a sanctuary lamp, being at home and at ease only at Mass on a Sunday, and feeling lost and at a distance when illness or work prevent; like smiling instinctively when you see a nun, bowing the head without thought at the sound of the Holy Name, and the strong, definite, and sometimes accepted impulse to genuflect when moving into a row of seats in a movie theatre.

Then, not the least of the joys of the Faith is that there is such a phenomenon as Catholic weathers. This is a difficult and subtle variation of our thesis, but if you have lived the glorious adventure of a Catholic childhood, explanation will be much easier.

Gray clouds, low in the sky, sudden wind and the whirl of brittle leaves is the weather for the Dead, the faintly frightening but always impressive season of All Souls. Crisp, clean snow shining with impatience and promise is Bethlehem weather. But humid August with the whine of those tree insects coming through the stained-glass windows, opened now on a swivel, is Low-Mass-no-sermon weather when a draft billows out the priest's green vestments as he turns. I insist that it is the weather itself that has Catholicism in it, by a kind of mysterious and appropriate sympathy that never is wanting, and never quite fails.

Uncertain, half snow and half rain, but with too much snow, desperately striving weather, what is that but Lent? And so it remains till the end of life. I should imagine that someone who once lived the Faith and then lost hold would be fretted by a deep and unrealized lack that would be in him like an ache impossible to name. It would be the weather that had become unsanctified with lost significance. His soul would miss the familiar, repeated, and identically worded pulpit announcements that tell of these events. But how could he miss the weather, and the constant announcement of the changing days?

And now, with unexpected and generous warmth that comes like a miracle, now, with the fresh newness over everything that grows, now, when the threat of chill is forgotten like a cloud that has run behind the horizon, in this unworn, this clean time, we have come to the weather of Our Lady.

These are hers, these days of Spring, and they cannot be mistaken. There is a kind, mild expansiveness about May, a sort of knowing kindliness and permission, rather like the slow smile of charity which is most deeply in the eyes, an understanding and a tolerance because all is well. These translate the weather of this month into the Mother of Christ. It's all mixed up with the fact, for instance, that going to Mass on the weekday mornings is not now the stern determination of Lent. This is softer, more filial.

Parts of all this are the reckless, spouting lilacs that will be spilled before the month is out. You can't convince anyone who has ever been a Catholic child that these lilacs were intended to wither on trees: they were meant, both the white and purple ones, to droop in profusion on May altars. A May hymn ripples the grass and whirs with the lawnmower, out for its first use, when people are sitting on porch steps because it's too early yet to bring out the furniture.

The weather is of Our Lady. The rain is more pleasant, and the puddles keep blue reflections, and dry up quickly. It's even too early for thunder. The ring of the baseball bat is in it. In the leagues they speak of the "crack" of the bat, but in the game on the corner, the bat rings with a resonance and satisfaction and triumph that never get into the leagues. She must love the corner lot, Our Lady, and the thump of a fist in a catcher's mit. It is her weather, and this is her kind of bliss, and she must have watched something in the long ago not too unlike this game?

So the raking of the leaves, not in resignation, but in preparation for sun and warmth, the surprise of violets in the grass, the plans for clearing and cleaning and painting, the first sweat from the sun, the first dust scuffed up in a schoolyard. . . . Our Lady's weather in the Mary, Mary month of May.

FRANCIS THOMPSON AND THE MEDAL

APART from the Rosary and the Scapular, probably the most common sign of a devotion to Mary, the Mother of Christ, is the little medal known as the "Miraculous Medal." It is worn and cherished by millions of people. It is made into a jewel, and hangs in mere tin around the shoulders of tanned children yelling on a bathing beach. It is always a good sight. It is like a badge, an emblem, like some multiplied and widely shared decoration in a spiritual nobility. All over the world it is like a sign of membership in a heavenly club, and it is worn for identification.

The figure that is cast on one side of the little Miraculous Medal is familiar to the millions who wear it. Our Lady stands on a globe, and her hands are spread in a gesture of bestowal. Rays, as of light, stream forth from her hands, and the millions know that these represent the grace which comes to us from God through her. It is a familiar portrait, that of the Medal, and we might wonder how familiar it was also to Francis Thompson as he dreamed his magnificent poetry in the London of the last century.

There is no question of Thompson's devotion to Our Lady. He, who wrote the "Hound of Heaven," the "Lilium Regis," worthy of re-reading now that the Church is under such violent persecution, and the "Ode to the Setting Sun," surely loved her well. We have his tributes to Mary scattered throughout the poems. We have Thompson's lines in "Our Lady of the Night":

> She sums all virtues that may be
> In her sweet light of purity.
> The mantle which she holds on high,
> Is the great mantle of the sky.

Surely, he who returned to God from a gutter, knew Our Lady's care.

But we may wonder in addition whether Thompson took to his heart that figure of Our Lady with her hands spread and with those rays streaming down to us all. Did he, the poet, ponder that? Did he dream of it, or did he write of it independently, and by a movement of the grace of God? For write it he did. We find his words in the dedication of the "Sister Songs."

The passage comes near the end of the dedication when Thompson was asking for help in his task. "Be aidant, tender Lady, to my lay," he pleads.

> Who from thy fair irradiant palms
> Scatterest all love and loveliness as alms;
> Yea, holy one
> Who coin'st thyself to beauty for the world!

It is an impressive description. It exactly fits what millions of people wear around their shoulders. This is our Miraculous Medal in poetry. Those few lines constitute one of the finest tributes to Our Lady in the English language. "Who from thy fair irradiant palms . . . scatterest all love and loveliness as alms . . . who coin'st thyself to beauty for the world!"

We must omit any comment on the "irradiant palms" in contrast to the nailed palms of the Son, and any comment on that profound word "alms" in reference to "all love and loveliness." But let us, at least, note the last phrase, "who coin'st thyself to beauty for the world."

The beauty of Our Lady is a moral beauty. She is, indeed, the face and the form that looks out at us from the madonnas of Raphael and Murillo and the rest: she is, indeed, the figure in the Michael Angelo statue. But the beauty of Mary is a moral beauty. She gave herself totally to God. She said, *"Be it done to me."* She was dowered with the fullness of grace. The loveliness is in the Immaculate.

And Thompson says . . . "who coin'st thyself." Of course it was the soul and the will of Mary that achieved, with God's grace, the beauty which is moral. It was her own consent. It was her own dedication, and it is a far distant, but identical task that each one of us has. Each and every soul alive must coin itself, stamp itself, engrave itself to beauty, and give itself to beauty, and give itself to God. Thompson knew the source of Our Lady's singular and unique pre-eminence with God. He wrote precisely of that when he wrote these lines.

It is the same source that must design the lesser beauty in the souls of us all. "Who coin'st thyself to beauty . . ."

OPEN HOUSE

VOCATIONS to the sisterhoods do come from God, they are the inner concern of an individual soul; and no Catholic, much less a priest, would dream of trying to create artificially a desire to enter the convent. That is a matter between a young girl and God. A vocation is indicated by signs which the girl herself, with counsel, must read, and the signs are these: a normal Catholic sanctity, a balanced and poised personality, a normal ability of mind, freedom from any unusual obligations in the world, love of God, a liking, even though vaguely perceived, of some branch of a Sister's lifework . . . and there are many varieties . . . and the notion that a life spent for Christ could give happiness, a satisfaction to existence, that would be lacking elsewhere.

There may well be some indecision about it; there is puzzling about everything, even in deciding on a job in business, and even in a lesser romance than the love of Our Lord; there is always wondering. A real vocation to the convent need not demand the blazing visitation of an angel, nor the loud thunders of another Sinai. It's all very human and it happens in the human way.

Often it seems both the general attitude of the world and of some Catholics to discourage, and perhaps *prevent* vocations to the sisterhoods. Often there is not the same reaction in the family of a girl who thinks she might be a Sister as there is in the family of a young man who thinks he may be a priest. It is obvious that a priest is getting into something that is a career; it may seem that a Sister is losing everything in a blackout. We seem to have heard the expression, "bury herself in a convent." Also there is something about "convent walls," which phrase has about it faint overtones of a feminine jail.

This sort of thinking is stupid nonsense. A Sister does not lose when the veils are put on. She gains. She wins. Presuming she is fitted by grace and adaptability to community life in the chosen field, teaching, nursing, study, administration, whatever it is to be, there is open to her a great, rousing, permanent, and very enviable happiness for all her days. This is a life worth what is put into it. This is a career for Christ in the long pageantry of the Church of Christ. Certainly bad days will come, certainly the ache of earth will be felt, certainly there will be ups and downs, certainly it will hurt often, and certainly there is real sacrifice here. Does anybody escape such things?

Sisters are people, and dullness, nerves, fatigue, worry, routine, happen to them as they happen to the rest of the human race, and Heaven must wait; but in a convent is high and enormously satisfactory living, for Christ is justification even for the planning of a third grader's lesson. Our Lord is the reason for keeping the laboratory chemicals in order, and Christ is the reward for every labor in every day. I dislike very much the coining of cheap phrases to catch attention, but maybe I can say all this quickly by noting that it is really true for the Sister in the school that Christ is the Principal and also President of the Board: the Sister who nurses works in an office where Christ is the Doctor: in every job He is the Boss.

Just a few things more: probably some of the attitude in some homes and in some people towards the Sisterhood is due to the fact that the English word that translates the Latin term for Sister is the word "nun." I claim there is something harsh sounding about nun, just as there is something harsh in calling a convent a nunnery. Nun sounds like none. It almost seems to be slang for nothing. This is unfortunate because the reverse is true. A nun is not none; she is, rather, all . . . for she has all in Our Lord. It might help if we adopted the practice and spoke hereafter of "Betty O'Gorman who's gone off to be an All."

I hesitate, in honest ignorance, to mention the habit, or uniform that Sisters wear. I do confess the wisdom and the grace that is the Rule. But if the case were judged by reality rather than Rule, then the world at large would see Sisters moving about dressed in all the colors of the rainbow, glorious golds, crimsons and blues, fuchsias and vernal greens, in everything in fact except dull gray and black. They would rival the celebrant at a Solemn Mass for brilliance in the vesting. They would look what they are, for, to paraphrase just a little:

> The nuns go robed in rain and snow
> But the heart of flame within.

Once on the occasion of the formal opening of a new convent, the Sisters invited the parishioners in to celebrate with them over a cup of tea and a cookie. That might be a good idea generally about once a year for all convents. Everybody could see then. There is an ice-box and a stove in the kitchen. The cloistered, or private, section of the building has real beds and chairs, and rugs are on the floor, and there are radiators in every room. There is a radio in the community room which would imply that the news, the Metropolitan, and much music could be heard if Sister were in the mood. It is all quite normal, quite human. And there is a chapel where Our Lord always is, and this is the Sisters' own.

HEADLINES

It has been claimed, and with obvious justice, that watching the movies is an acquired skill. The movies are something that no man can enjoy through his natural talents. You have to learn how to follow them. This interesting theory declares that an unsophisticated, innocent, and inexperienced soul who had never before witnessed a motion picture, would be able to make neither head nor tail of the simplest performance. Of course, we all learned the trick in childhood. Most people are expert. They can watch the close-up, the huge focus of the hero's face, the panorama of the city street, the cut-back to the front parlor, the shot of feet walking upstairs, the close-up of a baby crying, and a final fade-out in a sunset, and with these make a connected story out of the whole business. But it has to be learned. There are premises, conventionalities, methods, techniques which an audience concedes to the movies. Without the conventional knowledge on the part of the audience, the movies would merely seem to jump like photographic palsy.

Now, I would argue that the same sort of acquired skill is necessary to read the headlines in a newspaper, especially the headlines on the sports pages. Unless you grant the sports pages certain privileges in your mind, they read like the wildest fantasies ever put in print. Once there was a man who had not yet lost his mind, but he had lost his habit of conventionality. He approached the sports page, not with the accustomed permissions given to the editor, but with a plain, literal interpretation. It was terrifying.

It seemed that a group of Indian rulers, the very leaders of the tribe, had caught some monstrous human being with two heads. They had gathered in a circle around a flock of twittering birds. They held up the poor two-headed victim by his heels. Then they dropped him to the birds, presumably so that the birds would destroy him and thus relieve the tribe of disgrace.

Horrible, isn't it? But it was all in the headline, and I quote: "CHIEFS DROP DOUBLE-HEADER TO ORIOLES."

It seemed that some outlaws still infesting the high seas had been playing cards on their evil vessel. But they could not find the three of spades in either of the packs they were using. So they all ran to the starboard railing and violently threw the packs over-board, first one pack and then the other. Then somehow, in a miraculous fashion, the missing three of spades was restored to them. I don't know what they did then. I know not whether peace was restored on the plunging vessel, or whether the out-laws climbed to yard-arms to yell and scream in triumph.

I yearn to know what happened, but I shall never find out because the headline merely said: "PIRATES DOWN CARDS TWICE TO REGAIN THIRD SPOT."

A gang of muscled, tall and ferocious people, possibly four or five of them, at last feel safe from the threat of the feet and the heads of two children born almost in the same moment. Both of these children were named William it seemed. They had threatened for a long time and the struggle had been arduous. The feet and the heads had been dangerous. But now there was safety. The tall, ferocious people were safe. William no longer threatened.

No wonder I heaved a great sigh of relief in the sudden Spring warmth for the headline revealed: "GIANTS CONQUER BOTH ENDS OF TWIN BILL.

Do you consent? A literal mind can make the sports page into a nightmare. A literal mind can do the same with the movies, but I am concerned here only with the headlines.

Admittedly there are milder and more soothing things to be learned from headlines. For instance, you can discover that for once in history "BETTER SELF WINS RACE." However, it really is a let-down to learn that Better Self is a horse and not a man, and that the race where Better Self won was on a track, and had nothing to do with morals. In morals the headline should read: "BETTER SELF OUGHT TO WIN." But like most pre-dictions, in racing as in morals, it won't come true except with a lot of prayer and effort.

Sometimes the headlines are not horrible, or thrilling like the Better Self headline, but only pitiable and a source of great sympathy and tears. There is the case of the poor man who had been wandering hopelessly through the desert in search of water. He went from spring to spring, but they were all dry. He was exhausted, a miserable sight. All his perseverance, all his sheer and stubborn will to live have failed him. He can find no water, and he "FALTERS AT 30TH HOLE." To you a golf match; to me, a tragic and epic story.

Since it is Spring, the usual schedules for the athletic contests in the schools will soon begin. I shudder. Suppose this literal mood, this plain-reading mood continues. What then will the sports pages be like? What indeed? Good St. John the Baptist will wrestle with St. Patrick. St. Anthony will wallop St. James. St. Bridget will trail St. Lucy, and St. Vincent, he of the charity and the orphanages, after long years, "TOPPLES CATHEDRAL." But it could be worse. Holy Angels could defeat All Souls and that simply could not be endured.

HEAVEN IS NOW

ONE of the more tiresome communistic slogans used to be: "Religion is the Opiate of the People." Apparently it is not current any longer since those bureaus which do the thinking seem to have changed the attack, but the phrase once was as incessant and as annoying as an itch. The opium of religion was supposed to induce dreams of Pie in the Sky, and through this nebulous vision of a future reward in Heaven, distract the victim from the real and very present problems of the world.

But although the Communists have dropped the Pie in the Sky nonsense, you can frequently discover quite the same attitude in many other, non-communist, references to Catholicism. Some people do have the strange notion that the benefits of the Faith are only to be gained after life has ended. They seem to have the impression that religion is an arduous burden, a difficult and unhappy task, that it is endured only because you win a prize at the end. Omar, in his blunt, pagan way, advised his readers to "Take and cash and let the credit go," and he has many spiritual disciples who regard the earth and all its frenzy as cash indeed, and religion as a rather speculative promissory note.

Now the whole teaching: "*My kingdom is not of this world*," and the undeniably obvious doctrine: "*We have not here a lasting dwelling place*," are basic to religion. Heaven is very much part of the plan. The Pie in the Sky and the assumption that Heaven means "anything you want for free" are pretty childish, but it is still true that Heaven is what we hope for. Heaven is the fulfillment of the human person in the measure of his own capacity. Heaven is the purpose for which the soul was shaped, the possession of God in Love, and in a happiness beyond experience or description. Heaven is to be had for the earning, thanks be to the good God.

But it is a mistake to think that all of the endowment of religion must wait for a future. Catholicism begins Heaven here and now. The rewards are immediate, a matter of daily enrichment, and we ought to note the simple fact that non-religious living, so prevalent in our times, is thin, shallow, and petty when compared to religious living, and that lack of depth and size is its chief characteristic. The Faith actually gives a bigger life to live. Remove the Faith, or narrow its practice, and life, this week, this month, diminishes. Anybody can be glad when it is May; the Catholic is glad with the added joy that May means Our Lady, and the inner, half-secret happiness that is the sound of her name. The lilacs take on an air of tribute, the fresh blossoms acquire a spiritual significance, and the brighter mornings mean more than springtime.

Night prayers and the bedside examination of conscience are more than duty; they indicate that this casual, anonymous day contained adventure, and that it is filed away as part of a total story. Without religion there would be no story, and if no story, then no hero running risks, conquering hazards, winning triumphs. The Sunday Mass is not just an obligation; it means that you do count in the vision of God, that you are an individual, and that you are important enough to be missed, even in the presence of vast crowds, if you are not there. You have a place in the scheme of things, and the place is your very own.

Certainly the Catholic enjoys the trout stream, the lazy leisure with the Sunday papers strewn about, the late sleep, the sunny fields of golf, the ride in the car, the day with the children, but all these are twice as much fun if they are not alone but rest on the solid foundation of the worship of the Mass. What ought to be seen is that for the Catholic, Sunday is not just the papers and the day off, not merely a break in the routine. Sunday is that . . . plus.

I have nothing but sympathy for newspaper reporters, and especially for those reporters who write for the society pages, but I have often observed how helpless, how inept, how trivial the society reporters are when they must describe a Catholic marriage. There the story is, with perhaps a photograph of the bride. The out-of-town guests are carefully mentioned. The gowns of the bridesmaids are described. The list of all relatives is included. The name of the church is printed, and the variety and the placing of the bouquets are given in detail. That's all there is. The whole wedding, by description, is no different from a wedding that takes place in a hotel parlor, in a city hall, under an awning on the clipped lawn of an estate, or in the Hollywood manner. The papers report the trimmings; they miss the reality.

This is a romance that religion has ennobled and deepened and made rich. Here is the union of two souls helping each other on the way to Heaven. The words, "until death do us part" have glorious honesty in them. This man and this woman belong to each other. There will never be other flowers, other lists of bridesmaids, other pictures in the papers. This is a vow . . . forever. The pledges are enshrined in a Mass that is their Mass, in

a Holy Communion that is *their* Communion. Christ is here as
He was at Cana. Divorce does not lurk like a blight in the background. The current one-out-of-three percentage has no dismal
threat here. This is not tentative, nor half-hearted, nor fragile,
and there is quite another blessing than the wistful saying of
"Good Luck." Religion is the main theme of a Catholic marriage,
and it makes all the ribbons and the laces and the society reports
look just like ribbons and laces and society reports. The Catholic
wedding does not depend upon them.

And the abstinence on a Friday is not just a small observance of
a small ritual. The Faith puts meaning in one day of the week
as Christ put meaning in one day in all time. Meat on Friday
would be as dust in the mouth. St. Christopher rides in a car;
Our Lady's medal is worn like a badge; religion adds retreats to
conventions; and religion puts a Missal in among the books of the
month that the clubs select.

We could continue. The Faith has quite a lot to do with actual
living, and I suppose the genuine Catholic rarely thinks of Heaven
at all; at least I am sure he never thinks of it as the sole reward
and justification for his life. The Faith gives too much now.
Heaven is the last great endowment, but it is not waiting all by
itself.

A child has an immortal soul behind his laughing eyes; the three
meals are salted with the Grace; the calendar turns from Feast
to Feast, and Season to Season, in the liturgy; and death has the
great Requiescat to give it peace.

SISTER MARY JOSEPH

Sister Mary Joseph of the Holy Child rejoiced both in her
vocation and in her name. She rejoiced in her vocation for it was
the teaching of religion to children. Other Sisters of her Order
were nurses, English scholars, biologists, administrators, teachers
of mathematics, and Sister Mary Joseph of the Holy Child recog-

nized the simple fact that they all served God and the Church indispensably in the scheme of Catholic education. And yet, she was glad that she was permitted to teach Christ, and the Sacraments, and the Commandments directly and exclusively. This was what she could do well; this was what she was ordered to do every day in obedience. It seemed a very happy arrangement of Divine Providence.

She rejoiced in her name for, obviously, she was, in herself, the whole Holy Family: Sister Mary Joseph of the Holy Child. Wherever she went it was like the Flight into Egypt, except that it seemed to her a little spectacular to think so, and she preferred the quieter meditation that wherever she went, she brought Nazareth. Her name, as her vocation, was a source of endless joy, and it was a constant incentive in her work. Secretly she thought that even more than Sister Angelica, or Sister St. Thomas, or Sister Prudentia, her name was one that demanded of her all her energy and the best resources of her teaching skill. She was not at once Sister Mary and Sister Joseph and Sister of the Holy Child without a certain significance in her daily tasks.

But when it is said that Sister Mary Joseph taught religion to children, and not sociology to adults, and when it is said that she rejoiced in her name and her life, it is not said that she had an easy time of it. Contrariwise, she worked very hard and very long. With her Sisters, she circulated in the country conducting classes where there were no schools. She had to keep whole sets of lists of names. She had to be a school in herself. At first the convent automobile seemed to suggest an uncloistered and reckless freedom, particularly since she usually sat with Sister Chauffeur in the front seat; but she came to understand that the automobile was as necessary as her catechisms and books, and as tiring as standing at a blackboard. The Ford was part of her long missionary day, and its speed figured in the close schedule of her many and distant classes. Sister Mary Joseph knew joy in her work, but it was work, and it brought fatigue.

Doubtless it was the fatigue that made her dream the dream on that night in June. It was not a worry dream. It was not a troubled dream. Afterward she decided that, dream or not, it was part of her life. It was a happy dream.

She seemed to have traveled a great distance, which may, of course, have been the unconscious influence of the convent automobile. She was far away from her home in a place she could not recognize. There did not seem to be any scenery, nor indeed, much of anything. Only space. Huge, immense space was all about.

Then suddenly she saw the Bleachers. She knew they were bleachers both from her previous experience in a Catholic High School, and from the time she attended the Eucharistic Congress which was held in a ball park. There they were, unmistakably bleachers, but Bleachers to dwarf anything to be seen on earth. Tier after tier they stretched into the sky; row on row they reached across the horizon. She couldn't see to the top; neither could she see the end on either side. The space was full of Bleachers.

And the Bleachers, so Sister Mary Joseph of the Holy Child dreamed, were full of Angels. Thrones, Dominations, Powers, Cherubim and Seraphim, rank on rank, crowd after crowd, all the Angels of Heaven were sitting in the Bleachers. That was why she could see neither the top nor the sides. Nobody has ever limited the Angels to numbers or to space, and certainly Sister Mary Joseph would not even dream of limiting them to Bleachers. There they were, each a species in himself, all the Angels of Heaven.

She had no time for any emotion at the sight, neither joy as was her habit in waking life, nor excitement which was her attitude towards any crowd, because instantly one of the Angels in the bottom row spoke to her.

"Come, sit down," invited the Angel.

Sister Mary judged he couldn't be Gabriel. Not with that offhand manner.

"Oh, no," said Sister, "I wouldn't think of sitting. I'll just stand here quietly, if you please."

"Stand nothing," the Angel replied. "You are Sister Mary Joseph of the Holy Child, aren't you? Well, then, you rate a seat right here in Row A in the Cherubim Section. Sit down. It's the Season, you know."

"The Season?" questioned Sister.

"Yes," answered the Angel, "the Season. It lasts for three or four weeks according to the way you compute, but to us it's very brief, and we don't mind sitting through. A thousand years are as a day, you know."

Sister Mary felt reassured for the Scriptural reference, and sat down. He seemed a rather friendly spirit.

"Yes," the Angel went on, "it's the Season. You see, we Angels were created to adore and enjoy God in Heaven . . ."

"Oh," said Sister Mary, sitting up and all attention, "I know that." This was an Angel who knew the catechism about himself as well as the Scripture, and she was as pleased as she would have been at finding a bright child in one of her classes.

"And," the Angel continued, "during the Season the Good God lets us sit here and adore Him by watching. This is First Communion Season; furthermore, it's part of Confirmation Season."

"I know," said Sister, feeling that she was getting on quite well, "this is June. Pentecost and Trinity Sunday and all."

"Exactly," the Angel smiled in his thoughts. "The Season. We watch. Look over that way where we are all looking."

Sister Mary couldn't see much of anything. It was as though the gray sky of a cloudy day had been reversed and stretched out where the ground ought to be. From the bottom row of the Bleachers, far away in the distance, all she could see was a vast, murky, upside-down sky, with no break in the clouds. The Angels were looking at it intently. Expectantly.

"That's the earth," Sister Mary's friend explained.

"Our earth?" Sister was surprised.

"That's one of the things the matter with it," the Angel added, "people calling it 'our earth' when it's God's. It looks all gray because it's shaded with evil. Sin, you know, is pretty dull. But watch."

Sister Mary Joseph of the Holy Child watched, as she was bid, and forgot entirely that she was dreaming. Soon the loveliest linked twinkle of lights gleamed like a quick chain of stars through the gloom.

"Ahhhhh . . ." breathed the Angels in a long sigh of pure joy. Sister Mary had never heard anything like it ever. It was like singing and the sound of strings plucked in a great arpeggio. "Ahhhhh . . ." breathed the Angels.

"Yes," said her friend, "it's beginning to happen. That was an early First Communion Class receiving Him. The linking of the lights is the bright new Grace He brings to their souls. Not a very large class. Only nine or ten I'd think. Probably a small parish where the priest had to have them early in the season. Watch. You'll see more."

Sister Mary strained her eyes. She couldn't bear to blink even a little blink for fear she'd miss a single chain of the lights coming through the clouds. So beautiful the first Class was. So like diamonds thrown up in the sun.

Then all over the gray, flat plain she saw the streaking, multiplying darting, in long chains, of stars that lit and gleamed and filled the whole vastness that was the earth. It was as if a dark night suddenly broke out in dancing constellations. They ran in necklaces to the West, criss-crossed up through the East, marched like light-children in procession through the center of the sky and towards the edges, wove, stitched, and interlaced in patterns of new light. She couldn't have dreamed such beauty. It was beyond dreaming, and if it were not true, could never be imagined. Sister Mary Joseph found herself singing as the Angels were.

"Yes," said her friend again, after his own burst of joy, "this is the Season of the First Communion Classes and Our Lord; let's watch the Grace He brings with Himself for their souls. It's one of the Lovely Seasons here too."

"But see," said Sister, after she was able to talk again, "those stronger chains of lights. Those larger stars of fire. What are they?"

"They are the Parents," said the Angel. "They follow the children on the First Communion Day. The priests must be finished with the children. Now the Parents are going, and the Grace in their souls is stronger and brighter because they have received Him many times. That's one of the good things about the Season . . . the Parents follow the children to Him. The Thrones and the Powers in the higher rows of Bleachers are especially fond of this manifestation of Him."

Sister Mary was still watching the lingering light of the later classes when the whole gray mass of cloud brightened as with a fire beneath it. The sky seemed burning with steady glory.

"Don't look away," warned the friendly Angel, "don't look away. It will get very bright. The whole space will be a gold in fire. But you can endure, even though you see from here. This is the Season of Confirmation too, remember. You are watching the light of the Holy Ghost in Souls!"

Time, in Sister Mary's dream, seemed like eternity, although the Angel told her again that she had only watched for one season. At length the Bleachers stirred as though the unimaginable crowd were about to depart.

"What are those single gleams of light?" Sister Mary asked, "those bright stars appearing in the gloom that are not linked and chained?"

"Oh . . . those," said the Angel at last, "those are the Baptisms. They go on all the time, only not in classes. Baptisms are usually one by one."

The next morning after her dream, Sister Mary was praying in the chapel, and getting herself ready for Mass and another day of teaching religion to the children, when she chanced to look up in time to see Sister Sacristan lighting two candles with a taper. Sister Mary smiled to herself. The candles burned like two stars in the morning. The Tabernacle lamp burned like the star of Bethlehem, and for the same reason, and she was Sister Mary Joseph of the Holy Child who rejoiced in her vocation and in her name.

FLORENCE

POSSIBLY many people notice each Spring the conventional newspaper picture of a kindergarten graduating class. The photograph usually shows a double line of babies sitting on a stage to receive diplomas, each child solemnly becapped and begowned. There is human interest in the group, charm, attractiveness, and that magic and innocent persuasion to joy which the sight of children brings to the heart. That, indeed, is why the newspapers publish such scenes.

But a great deal more is here than sentiment. More is involved than merely a local and parochial function. This is repeated in dozens of our schools. This has been going on for years. This is the tremendous, and almost miraculous, business of Sisters approaching the mind of a child and actually succeeding in getting inside the mind to make lessons clear, ideas plain, and knowledge secure. It's quite an achievement, and if you ever want to feel clumsy, inept, mute, and stupid, just stand up in front of any third grade and try to teach them something. With the eighth grade, it's easy . . . they know about language by then . . . but try it with the babies.

I recall much too vividly for comfort a furious attempt once made to explain the moral law to such a class. There were gestures and wild pawings of the air. There were subtle changes of voice and supreme pantomime. There was a cunning comparison made to show that the Ten Commandments were just like road signs. . . . "Road signs, you know, dear children," . . . and that we had to watch the signs carefully or we would be wrecked. It was a magnificent performance, and I retired from the arena feeling like a combination of Thomas Aquinas and a Shakespearean actor. At the next assembly I asked with confidence: "Now, boys and girls, what must we do to save our souls?" Yes, you are right. After violently wriggling his hand at me, the brightest boy in the row replied: "We must watch where the sign says no speeding."

This delicate skill in establishing communication with the mind of a child is in evidence, of course, in any primary teaching, and we ought to pay constant tribute to the enormously competent and generally unappreciated profession entrusted with schools. Historically only the ancient Greeks and the Irish had proper respect and awe for the teacher. Great skill is present in any teaching, but I am now concerned especially with the Sisters and the more difficult and more important job of teaching religion.

Religion is not a subject of blocks and crayons. It comprises ideas. The Unity and Trinity of God, the Divinity of Christ, the matter of Redemption, morality, eternal life, these are the beginnings of an understanding of religion. The Sisters use all possible means . . . one of them being in that picture of an infant graduating class. They use song and story, psychology, picture, the liturgy and the vestments and the ceremonials, blackboards, rime, repetition and a formula; and more than anything else, they use patience. It is a professional and skilled technique. To the vast gratitude of the pastors, to the contentment and joy of the homes, the Sisters not only approach the minds of the infants, but they make entrance and convey the knowledge. The Faith is actually taught: the children grow up knowing what the Faith is.

Many a mother and father will testify that they never really knew their religion until after the children began to go to school. Sisters teaching catechism have more students than are listed on the roll books. More goes on in the religion class than is realized. Eternity is here. Decisions are here directed that will not come up for years. The chance at happiness is given here, a sense of values, a source of lifelong strength.

This is the time of the year to realize the great achievement, for this is the reason of the First Communion classes. In Spring it is the privilege of a priest to be amazed at what has been accomplished in the heart of a child. There are examinations, not heavy and strict and formal, but merely an inquiry into what the child understands about the Eucharist and Our Lord, and human conscience and contrition. These children are only around seven years experienced in living. But they know. All over the United States, at this time of year, they know. They know almost as much as the theologians and the scholars. The essentials are there, the fundamental realities. Christ was God, and His Mother's name was Mary, and His birthday is Christmas. He died because He loved us, and before He died, He left Himself with us in His priests who bring Him again in bread as He once did, and said to do. We must make Him welcome when He comes, really comes, in Communion by being as holy as we can. The words are childish. The babies may lisp and be tempted to put their fingers in their mouths. They squirm about in the pew under the examination. But they know. The Faith has been learned, and all the centuries since the day of Christ have been swept away, and Christ is recognized by His own.

It so happened that a little girl, through a series of circumstances, was not in a regular class and had to be prepared all by herself and without the attending skill of a nun. We got along pretty well, however, due entirely to the young lady's tolerance. She was very patient and broad-minded about the lessons. We were on the topic of creation, and Florence had it clear that God made everything. "The earth?" "Yes, the earth." "The trees and stones?" "Oh, yes, and the animals and the grass and everything." "People?" "Yes, God made people too." "But Florence, why do you suppose God made people?" That called for a little thought. That wasn't so easy. After a meditation and a shrewd glint in the eye, she said: "Because He didn't want to leave the place empty."

It was a bit dubious for a moment as to who was teaching whom. Have you ever heard theology put that way before? In fact have you ever heard anything more simply profound? Surely, we straightened the details out, and made the point about human souls being the only creation, except for the angels, that can love God and be happy. We went on from what she said, but Heavens, what she said! That the universe is barren, that the earth and the skies are lonely, that everything is but emptiness except that the image of God in human souls be there to love Him and to serve Him. That human freedom and grace populate and fulfil a plan. That purpose and final intent are discovered only in the drama of a free soul. That in us is the meaning, "He didn't want to leave the place empty."

Could Florence have meant eternity too? I wonder what kind of teaching technique it is to shout with laughter, and then stare at the pupil with a jaw dropped and wonderment written all over the face. I must ask a Sister some time. But you don't hear the book of Genesis summed up that way every day.

PRAYER BEFORE EARLY MASS

Deep in the east the dawn is white,
Pale like Thy Face beneath the thorn.
High in the east the dawn is red,
Red like the Heart a lance had torn.
Deep in the east the dawn is white,
Pale like the Bread You bid us break.
High in the east the dawn is red,
Red like the Wine You bid us take.

Uplifted Host! Uplifted Cup of Wine
Cry within this morning! And the sweet,
Sweet pleading comes again that once was Thine
Upon a hill whereon no sun would shine!
O Lord, I know not if Thy Paradise
Will keep such moment for the wakened dead,
Nor any dawn to flame it in their skies,
But if the beauty that the east has worn
Be gathered still, and still be white and red,
Then in my heart a single prayer is born:
Lord, let me be wherever it is morn.

In Summer, in a burst of summertime
Following falls and falls of rain. . . .

THE SOUL OF GOLF

ONCE upon a Summertime one of the more spectacular professional golfers scored poorly on two holes in succession and eliminated himself from a national tournament, much to the dismay of the reporters. He was supposed to be a possible winner, and here he was, topping the ball, slicing, and missing half-yard putts like any duffer. "Golf," he sighed to the reporters, "golf is a humblin' game."

With thousands of my fellows who will never be listed in any national or even regional tournament, I confess that the professional expert spoke the literal truth. "Golf is a humblin' game." To remember golf in repose is penance. Merely to contemplate a five iron ruins pride. Humility walks like an invisible caddie by the golfer's side. Whatever else his faults, the golfer is rescued from arrogance, and his dreams run only to the sins that gave him a six when he should have made a three.

Meditating thus on the depth of the professional golfer's wisdom, turning over in the mind many glorious Summers on assorted links, reviewing the long campaigns, not against par but against 100, the thought naturally occurs that golf fosters many other virtues besides humility. I will argue that golf is a Christian game. I will contend that golf is an heroically Christian game. It may even prepare the practitioner for martyrdom, but there is not the slightest doubt that it cultivates noble and conspicuous Christian character, and that the angels smile over every bunker, and line the edges of every fairway watching the golfers being holy.

Let us take the basic virtue of charity. Charity may be lacking in the office, may be absent from the street, may even fail within the home; but charity is never lacking on the golf course, mutual, shared, flawless charity between man and man.

The first tee is crowded with people waiting to play. They are impatient and swing clubs in practice. They lovingly polish balls that cost ninety-five cents each. They watch you as you step up and prepare your own ninety-five-cent ball for the wallop. You try to look competent as you attempt a few preliminary swings, hoping you appear an undiscovered Bobby Jones. You finally reach the crisis and they watch, the whole crowd watches you intently. You produce a mighty dribble that rolls selfconsciously off to the right.

Do they yell in derision? Do they groan? Do these fellow golfers and Christian men howl to the skies in ridicule? They do not. The silence is like the hush in a monastery. They make no sound whatsoever. They do not grin. They do not scowl. And they keep to that beautiful, charitable silence of the saints. You pick up your clubs and follow after your dribble, and their prayers and benedictions go with you. Golf is a Christian game, and the holy ethic of let's-keep-our-big-mouths-shut is strictly observed.

You find such silence, such charity vigorously in practice again on the putting greens. Nobody even whispers as you prepare for your failure at six inches. Nobody moves. Your companions are careful lest even their shadows confuse your attempt. They stand afar off like publicans. They try not to breathe, such is their virtue. They hold the pin that you may see. They may even pray with you and, indeed, you can observe the palpable presence of prayer and hope and much sanctity on the putting green. When at last you have missed the cup, they only murmur in consolation and protest against the bad fates that haunt you. Never in a lifetime of suffering with the putter have I heard the unkind word said. The putter moves men to exquisite sympathy.

There are popular and very false notions about golf and golfers. The canard is current that golfers lie about their scores, that they cheat and fail to count strokes, and claim achievement that is not earned. Any least golfer, any duffer, will refute this scandal instantly. The very reverse is true. Your golfer carries his actual score in his head like a conscience. Every stroke he adds to par is fearful to his mind. He cannot forget. He cannot fool himself. He is, actually, a paragon of truth, and as the saint examines his faults hourly, so the golfer examines his score card in true contrition and deep regret.

There is another false notion about golf and golfers that deserves refutation. I mean the mistaken and wholly tragic idea that golfers boast about their prowess. No greater misconception has ever hissed from the fallen mind of man. Golfers boast. Of course they do. They boast of their defeats, of their losses to par. They boast of how bad they are, and I swear to this out of the experience of a hundred locker rooms. Your golfer faileth not to accuse himself eloquently of his sins. He tells about his slices, and how he played all afternoon in the woods. He confesses to his three putt greens. He proclaims for all the world to hear how literally hopeless he is. That's how your golfer boasts.

I could go on and on in this Christian interpretation of golf. Perhaps anthems and poetry should be written of the game. Perhaps another Dante is needed to tell of Inferno, or another Chaucer to write of Tournament Tales. However, let us point out but two more aspects of golf. It is a game which yields only to orthodoxy. There is but one truth, one way to swing a club, one way to play, and that is the right way. Your golfer patiently works at achieving that one way. Heresy has no place in golf. Observe the good golfers, the men who are blessed with birdies, the experts, the sub-par heroes. You will find that they are all submissive to the truth of how a club should swing. They all stand in the changeless traditions. They are orthodox in a game that has no place for oddity.

Lastly, like every Christian incentive, golf is a game that demands active, personal participation. It is a positive thing, a practical and individual thing. Golfers don't sit in grandstands passively watching somebody else with a ball. Golfers do not recline on sidelines. Golfers do not struggle vicariously. They get in there and fight. They get in there and strive for perfection. They take themselves in hand and demand improvement in a personal battle against themselves.

Without benefit of statistics I should guess that there are many more people playing golf than there are people watching hired baseball players or tired race horses. Even casually tended courses seem to have half the population walking around on them on week ends.

In this country golf began as a rich man's game in exclusive clubs. It is not so any more. The game has become a democracy, and the sign of America is now seen in the overlapping grip and the stiff left arm. The only thing that is lacking is a good twenty-five-cent ball. Whatever happened to the twenty-five-cent ball? There's an issue that would sweep the elections any November.

AT HOME

WE COULD do worse in the midst of humid mid-summer days than consider the easy familiarity in religious matters which the Catholic would recognize in any situation, but which, somehow, never connotes either disrespect or lack of fundamental reverence, and which is far afield from the contempt which familiarity is said to foster. A good, devout soul need not be forever watchful of the solemnities. There is room in the Faith for ease and for what can best be described as an at-homeness. The awe before profound dogma remains, the sensitiveness towards eternity is not lost, indeed these attitudes are emphasized, but yet there does exist a simple, half-humorous, human mode of expression. Take the man preparing himself to attend the devotion known in most churches as the Holy Hour. In his usual fatigue over long prayers, he said that he was going down to the Holy Hour and a Half.

Anybody who has tried a long vigil will know exactly what the man meant. Nobody who knows what kneeling is would think that he meant the faintest irreverence towards Our Lord in the Blessed Sacrament. This is being at home, at ease in the Faith, and although it is slight, it is a genuine attribute of Catholicism. What the man really was saying was: "*the spirit is willing but the flesh is weak;*" that you pray even when you want to stop praying, that it does not matter if there is no sensed happiness in prayers, that even a saint may admit that sometimes an Hour seems an Hour and a Half.

This thought was informally expressed by a lady who had an exacting task to perform, and in her urgency prayed suddenly: "O, Mother Cabrini, you're a new one and not used to it yet. Help me get through this while you're still fresh at it."

Nobody who knows Catholicism would conclude the young lady here promotes the strange heresy that saints are subject to the weariness we feel on earth, nor is it to say that a new saint is livelier than an ancient one. This is neither flippancy or brashness. This is merely, and delightfuly, the old, blessed, familiar acceptance of very profound matters. It recalls the long experienced nun who said that the new saints were all very helpful, no doubt, but that as for her she would stick to Mary and Joseph.

There was once a parishioner I assisted at a moment when grief came in the death of a member of the family that had borne a long illness. The Faith was strong in the home, deep-rooted, and there was also a strong family bond. It is not easy, ever, even in the calm assurance of eternal life, to be separated from one beloved. Tears are honorable. Knowledge of immortality is not incompatible with mourning. This was a difficult time and it happened to fall near All Souls' Day in November. And so after the magnificent prayers of the Faith had been said . . . the "*Depart, O, Christian Soul*" . . . the "*Hail, Holy Queen*" . . . "*Nunc Dimittis,*" after the first grief, and after the inevitable, practical considerations had been argued, then simply, in those easier after moments when the fact of death has been accepted, someone said: "Well, I'm a little glad it is near All Souls. She'll be in time for the party this year."

Let us note that is not a light remark, that is not quite joking. Again, here is the familiarity that so gently presumes on the great girders of the Faith, on the great, timeless teachings, on the steady, solid truth. The Church exerts great effort, universally on All Souls. Of course there is entrance into the Presence of God. Of course there is heavenly rejoicing. It's all very real, so real that a Catholic soul may say: "I'm glad . . . she'll be in time for the party."

THE DAY OF THE CHAINS

IF A man deliberately were to attempt to say something which, of all things, would be the least startling, he might make a worse choice than to say that each day begins with a dawn and ends with a sunset. And yet, having succeeded in saying the thing that is the least startling, he would have uttered the one truth about the calendar which is most significant. Each day begins with a dawn and fades with a sunset. As if it were some rare, precious thing, the common day is found to be bounded with the splendor of horizon fire. There is an entrance and exit of dramatic flourish; Alpha and Omega of beauty; fire and blood-veined skies to begin, and vestment of martyr and cloud of flame to end. Of all facts this is, perhaps, the most observed and the least realized. It seems too common to be remarkable and, if in this red, repeated wonder, God is speaking silently to tell how great is His gift of hours, if these rays be His words, this light His language, this riot of color His rhetoric, in a Scripture never ending, the language is largely lost in a world grown tired of revelation.

For this world is a place of commerce and trade, and people of business can have little to do with sunrises and sunsets, and to them the recurring days have become but cold, efficient, numbered things. Thus on the ledgers, and through the neat files, you will find, for instance, that the day following Christ's birthday is simply 12/26/51. And the day of the harvesting is merely 10/8/51. Each day as it comes tumbling down the morning is given a set of digits, put to its grubbing task, and sent out again through the sunset, like a convict, nameless, unhonored, and numbered. 3/21/51 . . . you'd hardly recognize it as the day the miracle of Spring began!

But with the Church, the Church of Him Who was begotten before the day-star, there is a different kind of calendar, for the Church has made the dawn to be the time of Sacrifice and, in the sunset, she has, for centuries, said her vesper prayer. By an efficiency of her own, the Church gives each new day, as it comes, a definite name. It is set apart from other days by a kind of temporal Baptism, as a thing of dignity and honor. A day there is for Paul and Peter, and Timothy, and John. Other days are called for Vincent, and Martha, and Leo. The Church really becomes godparent for the hours. Days there are for Mary, special ones, fresh from the laundering of the Spring rains. Days for courage in a martyr; days for loveliness in a virgin; days for faithfulness in a confessor. The Church has seen so many suns rise, she has known so many sunsets, that in her mind she cannot help thinking of them as the drops of red that once fell from God's Son, and earned for all the saints the joy that their virtues ask.

And out of all the days thus gloriously named, there is a particular one, given back to God through Peter, who found his Roman prison chains had fallen away, and he was suddenly free.

On this day that marks the remembrance of Peter's freedom, something happened which was hardly as spectacular as the breaking of iron bonds, but which, still and all, was important enough. It happened not to a great man, as Peter is, but to a little woman, as Mrs. McEvily was.

Like the Church, Mrs. McEvily had seen many days, but unlike the Church, the days had made her old. There was a stiffness

in her limbs and in the middle of her back that made it difficult
for her to stand, so she sat, and rocked slightly in her chair, and
tapped the arm of it incessantly with her nervous yellowed fingers.
Her hair had grown thin and was pushed back in a grayed
remnant over her head. A little old lady she was, in the midst
of her troupes of sons and grandsons and all the in-laws and people
who tried to make her feel as if she must be ministered unto. The
lines in her forehead and about the delicate triangle of her face
were nearly always creased into an expression of annoyance.
People bothered her so, insisting on food and pillows and drafts,
when her soul was busy over the little loves that had happened
before she had come out from Ireland in the long ago, which was
but yesterday. Her eyes snapped at them, angrily, when she
lifted the cover of the lids, for her thoughts were flying, like
birds, over distant places, where her poor wrinkled body could
not follow. Some said it was a sad thing, and maybe it was, that
the mind and spirit that had braved so many worries, had prayed
over so many problems, had fought and pushed and fretted over
her brood, should, at last, be wandering, no longer concerned
over the present, but vaguely employed on its own lonesome
journeys.

Mrs. McEvily had no favorite granddaughter or eager child to
be with her. She permitted approach from no one. It was the way
the years had affected her mind, they said.

"Don't you want a little of the hot tea, dear?"

"Get out of here! Get out of here, I tell you!"

She spoke it with that incisive, precise emphasis on every word,
characteristic of some Irish speech, which can give such grace
to a blessing and such unshouting force to a malediction. "Get
out of here!" And the slight, curved set of teeth she suffered
to be in her mouth would knock with the sound of it.

It wasn't so bad that Mrs. McEvily should say this thing to all
and sundry in the household, but she also said it to the priest when
he called. "Get out of here!"

"But don't you want to see the priest, Mother?"

"No." And with her shoulder hunched, she drew away from him behind its feeble protection. "Get out of here!" To the priest!

Of course the family always explained what needed no explanation, and Father James K. Hyland, being a priest, only regretted that the poor tired spirit could take none of the gifts he held for its soothing. After the fatigue of life, there could be no Blessed Viaticum, no breathing away of fault in confession . . . the mind was gone beyond the power of seeking these things.

And so Father Hyland thought it a little sad that his possible ministrations should be made, in such great measure, impossible. He knew it was not always thus, even though he had not seen Mrs. McEvily when her wit was with her. He knew it from the kind of household she had fostered, where Christ's Cross was in all the bedrooms, Christ's Mother was on the walls, and Christ's grace was in the sons that kept the rooftree. He knew it from the very frequency with which he was asked "to drop in and see Mother, and don't mind, please, what she says to you." It had not always been "get out of here," when the priest called.

No doubt there was little essential need of his gifts for Mrs. McEvily's stalwart soul, but even so, sunsets are the finer for fanfare of splendid flame, and the fading of life, even of a life no longer quite rational, is the more glorious, if all the Almighty's Sacraments be well received.

The whole matter of Mrs. McEvily's wanderings of spirit was a source of worry to the household. She never said "get out" to the priest without causing a shiver of dismay to their souls, and they, being ordinary men, were not accustomed to the paradoxes of sanctity speaking in rebellion, and holiness making fierce gestures of rejection. They asked God for her release in morning prayers and in evening ones, and made sure that the priest should call at regular intervals, just in case she should decide to admit him. But the months were slowly counting on Mrs. McEvily now, and the years were closing in to smother the quiet beating of her heart . . . and all her thoughts were ever as the birds in the distance, fluttering over far places that cannot be seen.

Terce followed Prime, and None gave way to Vespers; dawns and sunsets came, and uncounted Masses were said. The leaves in the Church's calendar were turned; there were feasts and fasts, and Sundays and First Fridays . . . and then the telephone rang in the Rectory. It was from Mrs. McEvily's.

"Father, could you come? She seems better this morning."

An odd kind of summons. People usually said, "Can you come? She is worse." But this call wasn't usual. It was Mrs. Mc-Evily's.

Then down the street and up to the household of the sons, the priest hurried. Someone met him at the door and brought him to her familiar chair which still rocked and where the nervous fingers still drummed at the arm.

"Good morning."

The rocking stopped and the lids fluttered open. "Oh, good morning, Father."

"Good morning," said the priest and scarcely knew the truth he spoke. No petulance was here. There was a smile that lit the worn countenance, that seemed the more delightful because it was so unexpected. There was an unaccustomed light in the eyes; a strange lilt in the rocking and a quick folding of old hands that meant contentment and delight.

"This is Father Hyland," said one of the daughters-in-law.

Mrs. McEvily's smile was confident. "Of course it is," she said.

The priest turned and made a gesture towards the door. The son and daughter-in-law, and one or two of the grandsons who had come in childish curiosity at this new marvel in their grand-mother, quickly understood and left Mrs. McEvily and the priest alone.

"You feel better this morning?"

"Yes, Father, thank you."

The rocking of the chair grew quite rapid now, not in the

intense, preoccupied manner of the aged, but as if some joy had suddenly come to her and demanded motion as its only expression. From somewhere out on its restless voyaging, reason had returned and marvelously made harbor again. Some carelessly spoken sentence, the sound of some familiar voice, the appearance or touch of things long known, something or other, on this morning had contrived to reach out as a snare, and gently had made memory captive for a moment. The priest did not know, did not try to know the mystery of it. There the chance was, and what was to be done now, in this precious interval, must be done delicately and swiftly. The mind that had returned might as strangely leave.

"Wouldn't you like to make your confession, Mrs. McEvily?"

The smiling in the eyes continued. The head bowed slightly to consent. "Why, yes, I would. To you, Father."

The priest and Mrs. McEvily were strangers to each other utterly. Never before had she looked upon him with recognition, and even now, she knew not who he was . . . except that he was a priest, and to Mrs. McEvily, now that her mind was clear, there was no such thing as a priest who was a stranger.

The purple badge of the stole was laid quickly across his shoulders, his hand lifted in blessing. "Bless me, Father . . ." and the old remembered formula was unhesitating.

Confession made, brief and clear; penance given, slight, and of Mary's prayer; absolution granted, swift and dowered with Calvary's power; and the priest asked Mrs. McEvily to "make an act of contrition." For a moment the eyelids fluttered and the smile faded. "You know . . . say it with me. O my God, I am heartily sorry . . ." The look of uncertainty clouded deeper over her expression. Was the mind straining now to return to its distant places? The priest hurried carefully on to "amend my life. Amen," and Mrs. McEvily followed him in respectful obedience. And then when he had finished, taking not a moment to draw a breath, as if there were some hurry, something left out, something that this young man didn't realize was dreadfully important, the soft old voice of Mrs. McEvily, rushed on with her words:

> "For all my sins of mind and flesh, forgive me, O my God.
> For all my sins of speech and deed,
> For things I've done, and things I've left undone,
> Forgive me, O my God. . . ."

The priest couldn't catch the rest as the words hurried on. It was a kind of litany of sorrows, a formula of contrition, learned years ago, when this enfeebled mind was in its youthful strength and learning the deep matters of the Faith. Speaking out now, after all these years, was the instruction of some parish priest who taught a little girl in a church in Ireland. This was a part of Mrs. McEvily's very soul that was grooved and engraved with the doctrines of the Faith almost as firmly as it was sealed with the character imprinted at her Baptism. It was an expression of contrition. Complete . . . generous . . . annihilating! Before this barrage of sorrow, the minions of evil had learned to quake. Before this blasting onslaught, sins had withered and left a soul unhampered, and now in the uncertain days of her age, in this brief moment of rationality, her mind had found it again, and had hurled it over the ramparts. "Amen," said Mrs. McEvily. And the smile returned again as she looked up at the priest, apologetic for having interrupted him with his newfangled prayers.

But all the charm she was summoning to placate the priest for her moment of boldness was unnecessary. He was encouraged to go on with his ministrations.

"Would you like to receive Holy Communion now?"

"Yes, that would be nice."

The door opened, and one of the sons returned, eager to do whatever he could to assist in what was so unexpectedly occurring in his house. There was a little question about the matter of fasting, since Mrs. McEvily had already submitted to her breakfast, but the Church, the priest said, has special ways for people who are seriously sick, and since old age was a sickness, it would hardly be imprudent, in view of her years, to judge that Mrs. McEvily's sickness was serious.

After a few words and a few instructions, the priest left, and in a little while returned. But, he had been to the Place where the red flame is burning in the church, he had been to the Place where a Tryst is kept, *"till the consummation of the world,"* and he returned . . . not alone. The house of McEvily was a Tabernacle now, for He had come. The privilege of Zachaeus repeated and was new.

Candles were there, and linen, and silence, and kneeling sons and grandsons. A prayer was said and after the prayer, the great Annunciation of the Church: *"Ecce Agnus Dei."*

Mrs. McEvily instinctively lifted a hand to strike her breast, and the grandson, the youngest child, did likewise, and all that the ponderous theologies of the Schools demanded was fulfilled, for as the child, so the aged had seen that this Bread was Bread of Life, and Life Eternal.

No matter now if Mrs. McEvily's mind should take again to its wandering. It would walk along hallowed ways, her soul strong with the strength of a Guest it had welcomed.

Then the lids of her eyes closed again on the world at the bidding of the priest, and an anointing was made. The ears soon to be stopped to the noise of the world were brushed in Sacramental touch. The poor hands of Mrs. McEvily were lifted, and as she looked down upon them, through the tears in her eyes, she saw them sealed forever as Christ's with the signature of His Cross.

Really, the whole incident of Mrs. McEvily's reception of the Sacraments of the Church was not a spectacular event, since the gifts that she had received are a part of the heritage of the Faith and are as common . . . as common as death. Except that it was a little odd how her mind was cleared of the bonds of forgetfulness, so quietly and so momentarily (for on his next visit, the priest was told to "get out of here!"), the whole matter was very ordinary, and would be repeated to other souls as long as God is generous with His singular grace of time. Therefore, in the ordinary routine manner, the priest, returning home, sat down to enter the facts of the case in his sick-call record book.

For all the dull appearance that any record book must have, the sick-call record book of a Catholic Church is actually the daily diary of the Grace of God. In it, in every parish, are kept the names of those to whom ministrations are made, the record of the Sacraments given and the date of the call. In time, the book becomes almost an audit of the Divine, a roll call of the sick.

When Father Hyland began to enter Mrs. McEvily's name, for a moment he ceased to be the agent of Christ, and became a business man entering a transaction accurately and promptly. So, like a business man, he inscribed the date 8/1/51. And then he thought of something. What was that prayer the Church had in the Mass of this morning? "O God, Who didst loose the blessed Apostle Peter from his chains and make him go forth unharmed: loose, we beseech Thee, the chains of our sins, and in Thy mercy keep us from all evil." Yes, that was it. The dawn and the sunset of this day bounded a day dedicated to the breaking of a bond. So he scratched out 8/1/51, and for a date line over Mrs. McEvily's entry, he wrote: "The day of St. Peter's Chains."

———

THE ASSUMPTION

Once, towards Egypt, I conveyed the Way
On exile paths He could not walk alone;

And once I uttered syllables for Truth
To dwell in, when He sought beyond my womb
No other habitation for His own.

But if, through chaos, ye accept of me
His trinity of meaning, this be sign:

Build me of thy soul a lovely shrine
To keep the Life He gave me in a tomb.

DRIVE-IN

WEST of our town is an institution known as a Drive-In Movie which offers the possibility of witnessing a motion picture on a huge outdoor screen while keeping to the privacy of your own car. You drive off the roadway, pay the lady in the uniform, follow the signs, draw up through a ten-acre lot, take your place, fanwise, in the orderly rows, accept the loud speaker with its wire which is put in over the window, and there before you, gigantic, are the shadow antics of Hollywood. It is an experience, and nothing in the comment I now make is to be read as a complaint against the Drive-In. I wish it well and hope it prospers, and recommend it, especially as this outdoor arrangement eliminates the necessity of air-conditioning. In the Drive-In you get the pure, genuine air.

But to take a movie away from the dark narrow aisles, to lift off a roof and let the sky be cover, to broaden and widen a theatre until it is a field, a meadow, a space free to the stars; to do away with foyers and velvet ropes and lobbies and general confinement; to liberate the whole process in this fashion is to demand of assorted actors, male and female, more than they are prepared to deliver, either by script or illusion.

A movie seen against a last lingering of sunset must be a masterpiece, or it is a flop. They had better produce what they promise if the movie is to be seen outdoors. They must make them Colossal, Super-colossal, Tremendous, Stupendous, and each one will have to be fitted with A Climax That Will Leave You Breathless. Nothing else will do. It must be epic or nothing. This is an arena for Shakespeare, Milton, Beethoven, Rostand, Dante, and Barnum and Bailey. None of your three-bell stuff now. This calls for a three alarm. Mere Oscars here are not valid. In an outdoor movie they had better use Paul Bunyons for prizes. I suggest that somebody, perhaps Plutarch, sketch the ordinary lives of the actors who appear on this screen, and possibly Boswell for the intimate details, with Rabelais filling in the more spectacular outlines. The movie magazines should be mute here.

My own visit to the Drive-In occurred on an evening in July. It was a twilight for a poet's pen, and it must have been like this on the first, fresh creation of the world. A great, orderly, silent mass of automobiles was in attendance. Let me say again that I have no case against the Drive-In, but only a bewilderment as to how the movie industry is to live up to it.

The sight stirred the imagination. This field was not human. These cars were beetles, metallic-backed, actionless, regimented beetles intent on some biologic function supplied them through the veins that ran through to a central source. They were feeding. Nourishment, the substance of life, was coming to them. Now one moved, now another, by an instinct. The newly arrived came to the line and paused, content, silent.

This was like some primitive, ancient pagan rite. The huge, ornate bulk reared up to the West was an idol. These cars were bent forms in cruel worship. A gong might sound soon, and after it, the low ululation of fear. These backs were bared for a lash; the square screen was Moloch, god of stone.

It was difficult to believe that a lady named Betty was all that was about to happen. Betty, I think, and a boy named Jack.

When we finally were in place and waiting, the clear, vast light of the sunset was yet in the sky. Plainly we should have to be delayed until dark. Then horns began to toot, impatiently.

You could not see anyone except the immediate neighbor. You could only hear the anonymous tooting of the horns. Then, because the service is good, the loud speakers awoke to music. And then, O then, a movie flashed on the screen. It was in technicolor! The sky was blushed with gold, and far away the horizon was turquoised with silver. A single star hung in the heavens in such piercing beauty as Wordsworth mutely claimed for Lucy. The world was lighted in July glory! Never have I felt so sorry for Hollywood.

The technicolor was gray in contrast to the sky, the living heavens. Artifice and ambitions were failures. Pretense was now unmasked. If I were on the Board of Directors at any studio, I should make it a matter of contract that never would our technicolor process, achieved after long investment, be in contest with a sunset. The odds are too unequal.

The night came on and, with it, mystery, drama, the cool, ageless wonder of the world at dark when the harsh, too near certainties of day are softened, and all dreams and hopes are possible. The night came on and with it the "abashless inquisition of each star," with the "moon riding like a high peaked silver galleon set in ebony seas." As I say, the night came on, and then they turned on the feature attraction.

It seems there was this daughter of an English duke. She looked like any American girl, the duke's daughter. Her ambition was to get into a chorus-line to the amazement of Betty and Jack when they actually spotted her British calm. But they were good scouts and let her share a bun with them in the drugstore where there was no meat, or butter, or anything to make a sandwich with except hamburger which nobody wanted, and . . . You understand? It was not Shakespeare. There was no trace of Milton. Hollywood was not measuring up. Moreover, there was still the distraction of the night and the vast, eternal spaces reaching up, and up, and up.

The place stirred the imagination and I dreamed. In an off moment, right after somebody on the screen had remarked, "But I have the right to love," I dreamed.

In the dream a sudden pounding was heard. It spread and broadened until all the parked cars were filled with the noise of pounding. They were beating against the roofs of the cars.

Like men imprisoned they beat against the confining roofs. And they broke through. Now one, then another, they broke through the roofs that were like metallic-backed beetles. A hand reached out and bent back the steel. Then an arm, wildly striving, reached out, and the hole in the roof widened. Soon all the cars were broken and all the occupants were free. They all climbed out, breathed jubilantly of the night air, and sat there, out on the roofs of the cars and stared upwards, upwards towards the stars. The whole place was filled with people who were glad with a free, light-hearted joy, sitting out in the air looking at the stars.

THE SWAN POND

OUR town, which has a Drive-In Theatre to the west of it, has a Swan Pond in the middle of it. Dozens of automobiles stop at the pond every day, and scores on Sundays. It is exactly that, a Swan Pond, and regal on its surface, actual and plain, are four of those white, almost mythical birds. To children it must seem like a fairy tale set by the side of the road. The swans are not drawings in a book, not memories of Leda and Helen of Troy. They are not imagined: they are real, and they are there in the pond.

Probably the first discovery of people who drive out, or who, in delighted surprise stop by, is that the swans look like swans. They are all you'd expect them to be. The myths, the operas have not been fooling us. Swans are what swans ought to be. They demand symphonic music: they are majestic and graceful, and swoop for yards by one stroke while the head is arched disdainfully. There is but one word, gentlemen, and it is queenly. There is but one response, ladies, and that is awe. If you toss them crumbs, let the crumbs be cake. And if you feel inferior to these ruffed and spreading feathers, you only share the emotion of all other spectators. Merry-Go-Rounds used to have wooden imitations. That pond in Boston Commons still has swanlike barges. But these creatures are not *like* swans. They are.

The attractions are not done yet, however. In addition to the swans, there are the ducks. The ducks are not your waddling, barnyard variety. They are Mallards, wild, improbably colored, with green glossy heads, thin white collars, small orange feet, and shaped, in the underpart, in the fuselage, so to speak, like an Aztec vase turned on end. The ducks are a great contrast to the swans.

A swan is assured. A duck is belligerent. A duck is spunky. They are feathered Dead-End Kids, and likely, they are all named Donald. So there they are, slapping and sporting around the pond. The swans never notice them. But the people do. After a while the place seems more of a Duck Pond than a Swan Pond, which may be a sort of comment on human nature, on what stays interesting longer. There is a limit to the attraction of a pose. Even Ziegfeld had to liven things up with a comic.

So there are these ducks. They are not confined, and, indeed, come and go as they wish. They come in as if they were having the time of their lives; and there are people who swear that the quack before landing sounds like "Whoopee!" The orange feet are stuck out, and at an angle. They plow the water, and after a gay yard or two, let the body down, and then paddle like mad. When they get into full momentum, the rear tips up and the breast sinks in like a prow; the head is tilted, the ripples run out, and the gleam in the hard little eyes shines wickedly.

The very best of the show in this ex-Swan Pond is the moment when the Mallards dunk for food. It is a perfect surface dive. They submerge in their own length, and if the food is deep down, if it's hard to get at, then you have the precise illustration of the nature of a duck. The little feet paddle away in bursts of anger. At the tenth try they paddle harder than at the first. There is no water for them to paddle in: the feet are stuck in the air out of the water. But the ducks don't care. They are in there paddling. They paddle anyway.

It can also be a revelation by the roadside to observe the temper of the people who linger here. First comes delight. Faces relax and smile as they smiled in childhood. It is sheer fun to be close to the exuberance of the creation of God Who made both swans and ducks, *"and saw that it was good."* There is no artifice here, this is natural water, natural ducks and swans, and they have the power to make people natural too. It is simple human nature to be delighted with things; only the poor sophisticates have ceased to be impressed by what is under every sky and in every field.

The second reaction is not unrelated to the delight. It is an innocence. The joy that is here is pure, uncomplicated, primary and sweet. Nobody gains anything. The fun is innocent, and it is, in a very real sense, holy. Here by the roadside, near a busy and casual highway, is something of the spirit that moved St. Francis of Assisi to preach to the birds.

THE PROBLEM OF PETER AND PAUL

THIS is the problem of Peter and Paul. After we come to the statement of it, you may not think it is a very great problem. You may, indeed, conclude that the problem of Peter and Paul properly belongs to monasteries and convents and to people supposedly removed from the practical world. At the end you may admit that to ponder on it affords more refreshment of soul, more blessed entertainment of mind, more profit of heart than is to be found in worrying over the international situation or over the strange fate of geometry. The problem of Peter and Paul is very satisfactory in that once you arrive at your own solution nobody can offer effective debate.

To begin with, you must understand that summertime is the Season of the Person of Our Lord. It is one of the unrecognized seasons of the Faith, and by that I mean there is no public observance of a very thrilling and definite period in the evolution of the Church year. All the world celebrates the Season of the Birth of Our Lord. Everybody knows when it is Easter or the Season of the Return of Our Lord. Catholics generally are aware of the Season of Sorrow, or Lent, the Time of the Adorning, or the Immaculate Conception, the Time of the Victory, or the

Assumption, because these days are of obligation and many pulpit announcements bring them to our attention. But the Season of the Person of Christ is largely unnoticed, unrecognized and unenjoyed. A pity, but it is so.

The whole emphasis within the Faith in summer is the Person of Christ. He is always the Center, but now we are made to see that with special clarity. We are brought close to Him. It begins on the Feast of Corpus Christi, which is the Feast of the Body of Christ. The Mass and the prayers of the Church on that day are the same as in the Forty Hours. Corpus Christi is the Catholic world making a Forty Hours officially, and together. It is Holy Thursday all over again, and it lasts for eight days. Notice, as you must, that here the Person of Our Lord makes the Feast.

The very next Friday is the Feast of the Sacred Heart. The Faith does not delay, does not wait a moment. Immediately after we have been thinking of the Body of Christ we find ourselves in contemplation of His Sacred Heart and His overwhelming love of mankind.

But I forgot to mention that on June 24th comes the Feast of the Birth of St. John the Baptist. That, too, is part of the sequence and theme of these midsummer days. St. John the Baptist brings us to the Person of Christ because that was his reason for existence, his whole purpose in life. His birth was the guarantee offered by the angel to Our Lady that she would be the Mother of Christ, and John's was the announcement . . . *"Behold the Lamb of God"* . . . that pointed out the Person of Christ when Our Lord looked like any other pilgrim to the Jordan.

Let us not miss the nice implication of the Faith putting the Feast of the Birth of St. John just here near Corpus Christi time. John's words are repeated on every occasion when any soul approaches an altar rail. *"Behold the Lamb of God, behold Him Who taketh away the sins of the world"* is what the priest says as he holds up the Sacred Host for adoration before communion. John's language has been given Eucharistic immortality. John's place in the plan of Our Lord is permanent . . . he, through his words, is forever pointing out Christ. So there is no mystery and no problem as to why *his* Feast should fall during this Season of the Divine Person.

These days are a thrilling and definite period. On July 1st the Faith keeps the Feast of the Most Precious Blood. Again there is the same emphasis. This is the Person of Our Lord in the very action of opening Heaven for us. The Mass and Office for the day are like a review of all Holy Week. The Sacred Heart becomes the Wounded Heart. The Corpus Christi becomes the Body of Christ Crucified. The Lamb of God, we are bidden to behold by St. John, becomes the Lamb on the altar of the Sacrifice. And in this feast the choice of the rabble on the the day of Calvary . . . *"His blood be upon us and upon our children"* . . . becomes the universal prayer and plea of all men.

To make the theme of this Season utterly complete, July 2nd, the dawn following the Feast of the Most Precious Blood, is the Feast of Our Lady's Visitation. July 2nd is the Feast that remembers the time when Our Lady brought the Person of Christ to her cousin Elizabeth, and received the first recognition as the Mother of Our Lord. This was the day when Our Lady's heart overflowed in the Magnificat. *"He that is mighty hath done great things to me and holy is His name."* It is an echo of what every soul says in its most recollected moments; a pre-statement of what every soul should say at the end of a time which brings Corpus Christi, the Sacred Heart, the word of the Lamb of God, and the Most Precious Blood. This time has been another Visitation when the Person of Christ is near.

In the midst of all this the Church places the Feast of St. Peter and St. Paul on June 29th. It seems irrelevant to the sequence. It seems at variance with the theme. Why is this Feast set here? Why June 29th for Peter and Paul when they are also memorialized elsewhere in the Church calendar? That's the problem. Why?

I should not for a moment want to seem to suggest that Peter and Paul are out of place in the company of Christ. I do not mean to edge over towards irreverence or disrespect. I am not raising artificial problems here. This is no objection to Peter, nor is this any discomfort for the presence of Paul. I should not wish to think of them as intruders, or strangers, or saints who are somehow out of order. Yet there is reason for wondering.

Usually you think of Peter as the Founder, the Holder of the Keys. He is the name of jurisdiction. And usually you think of Paul as the Voyager, the restless, furious, burning Writer of Letters. He is a name of Catholicity. Why should the Church, when observing a Season of the Person of Christ, pause to include in the calendar's unfolding a special Feast for Peter and Paul?

It is not by accident. The whole function of the liturgy, the whole arrangement of Feasts and Masses and Seasons, depend upon the fact that the Church acts with purpose. You miss much of the meaning of being alive in the Faith if you think that all of this just happened. But why? Why Peter and Paul during these days?

O, come all ye of the Household of the Faith, come "ye who whilst living are marked in the sign of the Holy Trinity." Peter and Paul are the Church. You can't even mention their names, linked and allied as they are, without meaning the Church. Peter is the Rock: Paul, by the grace of God, is the Energy. Forever they mean the Foundation that is forever . . . the Church. And the Church is the Person of Christ. The Church is Christ extended through time, made contemporary to every age, available to every soul. Paul said that. He called the Church the Mystical Body of Christ. And Peter said . . . to you, and you, and you . . . to all members of the Mystical Body: *"Ye are a kingly priesthood,"* because all of us offer with an Ordained priest joined with the High Priest, Christ, the Body of Christ and the Most Precious Blood, on the altar of the Mass.

Peter and Paul mean that the Person of Christ is not a gift to be remembered because the Gift is past, but the Person of Christ is with us yet in the Church. Of course Peter and Paul belong in this season. The season would be incomplete without them. Feast days and seasons are not mere reflections we make to a distant past when Our Lord was among men; they are part of the living present. To be Catholic is not merely to recall in love and reverence: it is to live with Him, through Him, and in Him: now.

THE CAVES

THE whole matter of how blessed, how wonderful, how primary the creation of light is, hit me with full force when I ventured down into some underground caves, and with other subterranean tourists, explored them. These caverns are one of the wonders of the world, but they are under the world. You get into an elevator and go down into the earth the distance of some sixteen floors. Then they take you on a walk of about a half mile through bare, huge, rock caves which through thousands and thousands of years water has carved.

Electric bulbs are strung at intervals, and at one point in the tour, the guide throws a switch and there you are . . . in darkness! No natural light has penetrated here since God made the light. This is the pre-creation dark. This is the perpetual night. It is impressive, and you don't feel comfortable, nor quite safe. Literally it is as dark as Hell. Then they turn the electricity on again and you are amazed to discover how much of a support even artificial light can be.

The feeling is as old as humanity and possibly it explains why men always think of a fire on a hearth, or a light in a window as friendly. On the surface, in the elevator again, the operator was telling us to look up, and there we saw, glimmering, the real light of day like the promise of a Heaven over our heads. *"O ye stars of heaven, bless the Lord. Praise ye Him, O sun and moon: praise Him, ye stars and light."* You can understand what Daniel was singing about. A cavern in the earth can tell something fresh and magnificent about the common light of day. I should not care to go down in a submarine. Those fish that grow their own lanterns for the deeps, although God made them too, have always seemed diabolical to me.

I want to go on to say a word about the bravest, the most revealing, the most eloquent thing in the whole caverns, and it is not part of the caverns at all. It is a thing which would never be there were the caves not opened for exploration. There is nothing alive in the place. It is all stone and slime and chemicals and dripping water. The rock-lime formations took thousands of years to grow inches, but they grow by accumulating deposits, not by living. It is chilly down there; the constant temperature is around 60.

To guide the summer tourists, the management had strung electric bulbs, and there, clinging to the rocks near a couple of them, waving triumphantly in the artificial draft, were slight, green fuzzes of living grass. They had been there for about ten years, the guide told us. Some seed must have fallen or been blown in from the outside. Perhaps it was carried on the clothing of a visitor or workman. The bulb supplied warmth and light, and with only this for encouragement, life took root and grew! *"O all ye powers of the Lord, bless the Lord: O let the earth bless the Lord; let it praise Him and exalt Him above all forever."*

There is something out of Genesis in this sight of grass growing where perhaps for millions of years there was no grass. This is life, stubborn, unconquerable, obeying the laws of God laid down upon the universe since the beginning, and I told myself I was looking upon green grass as Adam saw it after he had been ten years made!

Thinking of this wonder of life it occurred to me that about all the young man, who was the guide, had to say to his party had to do with life also, even though it was pretended life. He did point out the roofs and the streams in the caverns. He was helpful with statistics and the history of the place. But, after all, a rock is a rock, which I for one, consider to be a better phrase than Gertrude Stein's "a rose is a rose." A stone is a stone, and a statistic is a statistic, and the business grows monotonous. About all you can say of a rock is that. It is a rock. To keep the interest of the tourists and to add variety and significance, the guide talked about living things.

He said that the formation in the corner looked like a man's face. He said that the formation on the wall looked like a turkey. Another one looked like a turtle. Another looked like a leg and a foot. The stones all looked like . . . like life . . . and the interest in them was the life they resembled.

That is a tremendous comment, given unconsciously, in a guide's speech for the benefit of summer tourists. The universe has meaning, the creation of God has significance to the human mind only because creation included life. There is no story without life. There is no adventure. The mental, the spiritual life, inside of a man, can discover what it really is by going down in a cave to find a world so lonely that the mere appearance of living must be produced by the action of the mind, and the power of the imagination.

One of the most religious and unexpected moments I have ever experienced came near the end of the tour when, as he had been doing all along, the guide pointed out an odd formation in a rock. "What does it look like?" he asked, and again the recurrence of that mental process of things lifelike haunted me. "What does it look like?" The crowd had many answers. "Like a sponge," said one. "Like cheese," said another. "No," replied the guide, "look again." Nobody guessed it. "That rock looks like tripe," said he.

Sure enough, it did. The crowd nodded. They were pleased. As they passed, they turned their heads to confirm the happy chance. Here, beneath the earth, in a dark and lifeless cavern was a rock that looked like tripe! Tripe is part of the stomach of an ox. *"O ye beasts and cattle, bless the Lord: O ye sons of men, bless the Lord."*

I left the tripe-rock reluctantly for I had looked on it with fondness. It was, by resemblance, the Sixth Day of Creation. Thank God, creation did not cease with the fourth Day or the Third Day, but went on, in God's Providence, to the real Sixth Day, and to the creation of men and minds and souls and the free human will which can claim Heaven.

The caverns would make a fine place to say a prayer; and if I were the local pastor, I should ask permission of the authorities, and organize all kinds of people in groups, from all nationalities, of all races, of all faiths and religions, of all ages. Particularly I should want teen-agers and children in the group. Then, with this cross-section of humanity, this group of men of good will, Gentiles, Jews, black and white, German, Irish, Russian and Chinese, the prayer in the deep caverns would be a prayer for peace. It would be a pleading prayer for peace, honest peace, among the sons of men, sons of the Creative God.

NEWS STORY

WASHINGTON, (UP) The Army and Navy are planning in advance for a vast network of underground military and industrial installations in the event of another war, it was revealed tonight. Military and civilian experts have been ordered to explore the nation's caverns for possible military use. The underground war centers would include such scenic spots as Carlsbad Caverns, N. M., Mammoth Cave, Ky., Wind Cave, S. D., and scores of lesser known natural cavities. An underground-sites committee has been established and it plans a complete survey of underground possibilities. . . .

The dark, damp hollows of the cavern echoed only with an occasional distant sound. A stone fell somewhere. Water dripped. A scurry of rodent feet was followed by a splash, and the noise of struggle in a flowing stream. Primeval furred life preyed on scaled and webbed life. There was no light here. Nor warmth. Only darkness and cold and mysterious sound after long prenatal silences. Wings beat against the stagnant air and then a rush of wings as bats blindly moved in search of other cliffs and ledges with thin cry and whimpering that died out to sightless silence again. Water dripped. A gurgling suddenly arose in dominance for subterranean tides, and then sank down again to drip, drip, drip . . . the cold, sterile, rock sweat of the cave.

The first sign was the quick flicker that touched the slime at the pinnacle of a stalactite. An instant only. Then it gleamed again and reflected to the long icy side of another. The bats quivered in alarm and swooped upward in the dark. Something threatened. They sensed it. Rat feet whispered in flight, and then stopped warily. Far away a buzzing sounded, followed by the metallic crackle of a radio. The winged flock wheeled and swooped. Light gleamed on the tall pinnacle of the wet stone and held.

"Party CX. Exploring Party CX calling communications. Calling communications. Corridor D ends in water, proceeding with searchlight craft. Follow with lines and trace marks. Over. Follow with lines and trace marks. East by northeast central level. Over." Then silence. Only the drip, drip, drip to the dark. A low, controlled, cautious rumble of an outboard preceded the beams of light stabbing through the cavern, seeking the rock edge, searching the roofs, the sides, the waters in slow, exact progress. The bow of the canvas boat stopped. The light swung again in circles. Water that had never shone broke to long reflections. Man had come to a cave.

Guide lines were set. More boats followed. The shouting echoed like a multiplied, repeating voice. Tripod floodlights were assembled and the whole vast plateau of the underground shelf became plain. The radio buzzed off. No need in the security of the landing and the location. Men were safe here. Safe from being lost to the main exploring party. They had light. And solid rock. They could trust to the power of their own voices. Their rubber-soled shoes found firm footing in a new place.

The exploring party had increased. Engineers measured with surveying instruments. Humidity, atmosphere were tested. The nature of the rock yielded to examination. Charts were formed, recorded, related to entrance and exit.

This was no mere hole in the ground. Industrial engineers calculated, searched, spoke together in satisfaction. Cost of construction would be low. No need for roof or siding. Water supply, air were good. Ventilation could be improved. "Why, there is floor space here for a whole radar appliance plant. Safety too. This is deep. Two degrees below the median with ample room for housing. A hundred huts could be built without crowding factory space, and Corridor D could be cut wider for tracks directly to Refrigeration and Food Storage.

"No. No. Tell Operations to leave the floods and all portable semi-permanents. Stay right here till Executive Planning comes in. This is only tactics now. Strategy is handed to us on a platter. Leave equipment. Cut the switches on all power lines. Prepare departure."

The dark returned. The waters under the earth lapped against the ledge quietly and came to a calm. Drip, drip, drip . . . the cold rock sweat fell in the dark again, touching a length of electric cable. A bat blundered against the smooth surface of a searchlight lens. But there was no light now. Man had gone from his cave. His was the only light and it would not kindle till he came again.

The details and the maps, of course, were top secrets, but the general notion that the caves were being prepared was considered with some satisfaction. In the Senate an oration rounded to a stirring period with words about "another of our great and God-given natural resources with which this nation abounds, made available to us by the unhampered advances of pure science without hindrance of creed or dogma and enhanced by the clear, hard-headed, practical thinking that does not lose itself in dreamy theory, but has the courage to take the liberal and realistic stand." Newspapers printed drawings speculating on cave locations throughout the world. A Sunday Supplement promised that science would, without doubt, discover caves beneath the ocean. There was a little argument among some of the columnists and on some editorial pages about the danger of a "new isolationism, greater, deeper, more dangerous than before," but hope was generally expressed that "this would be avoided by a prompt settlement within three years of the Spanish situation, and by the generous inclusion of Switzerland among the peace-loving nations." Some cry of "Fascist aggression" was sounded, and there was talk too of the "new, vertical, encirclement in depth," but on the whole a wide sense of security obtained which was not incompatible with an avowed trust in the UN.

No one paid much attention to her, nor indeed was she ever known to have given an opinion to a roving reporter, but after the news about the scientific accomplishment in the caves, a Polish Sister, cloistered in an Irish convent in Iowa, was worried. As usual when she was worried, she prayed. As usual when she prayed, she prayed not for herself. She never considered leaving her cloister, no matter how many atom bombs came. But she was worried because the people in the caves seemed to have all concluded that atom bombs must, necessarily, be *dropped*. True, they always *had* been dropped. Hiroshima. At that atoll in the Pacific. Dropped from airplanes. But they didn't need to be, really. They could be *planted!* They could be planted in the ground . . . secretly . . . planted in *caves!*

So the Polish Sister in the Irish convent in Iowa prayed. She prayed to Our Lord Who was born in a cave that was used as a stable. She prayed through Our Lady who, very possibly, hid and slept in a cave in the desert when she fled to Egypt from the wrath of Herod. And she lifted up her eyes because it came to her in her cloister that all the arching skies, all the spaces of the universe, only made a dark and abandoned cave, with neither Life, nor Light, nor Hope, except He be here Who is Charity.

"DO YOU KNOW FATHER O'BRIEN?"

SOMEWHERE in the novels of Bruce Marshall there is a paragraph describing the casual meeting of two priests who are familiar friends. Each tips his hat to the other, "saluting and recognizing the priesthood and the powers of the Holy Ghost residing in each one." I very much like the little incident because it illustrates the impersonal and sacramental character of sacerdotal grace. Priesthood is something that resides. It is something both independent and inner. One priest, quite without any selfconsciousness and without any pomposity, may tip his hat to another for each will know that the gesture is made towards an interior grace that exists forever, and that began when, at Ordination, each received a character altogether beyond himself.

To be sure there ought to be, and are, certain qualities of mind and disposition, certain disciplines, certain personal and human qualities to house the priesthood and give it fitting and less unworthy habitation. But these are not essential nor are they the premises. Priesthood is beyond any man's character. It exists in itself, for it is the gift of Christ and is the deposit of Himself placed within. I write of this glorious matter at the moment because a priest cannot travel twenty miles from home without vividly realizing it, and I have been afar for much more than twenty miles.

There are many little evidences that ought to be included in the saga: the airline hostess who offered a shrimp sandwich first and then, hestitatingly, a roast beef sandwich since she knew it was Friday: the very cordial and gentle Negro maid in the hotel who said with some pride of discovery, "You're a Father, aren't you?" and who for days was attentive and courteous, and who at last declared in the corridor with a bundle of towels in her hands that she was a convert of three years' standing and belonged to St. Thomas' where the old Father had died: the unknown priest seen on the street hurrying with the crowd who waves and smiles, or, if he is near enough, says, "Hi": the voice of the old pastor on the phone who kept saying, "Who . . . who did you say?" until identification was finally established when he said, "Where from?" At the mention of my home, he replied, "May the Lord help you," and that I was to call "when one of the assistants is here": and the quite natural assembly of the three Roman collars under the ramp at Ebbets Field while waiting for the rain to clear over the Dodgers: there are, as I say many little evidences that ought to be included concerning the impersonal and universal character of priesthood, but for the sake of space we must be limited to only two in detail.

The first has to do with the sacristy, or the vestry, in St. Francis' Church on 31st Street in New York City. That very busy and crowded church is adjacent to Penn Station and several hotels, and it offers traditional Franciscan hospitality. Many priests stop in there for Mass en route. There always seem to be enough altars and enough vestments for everybody, and I do not mean it as irreverence when I say that the sacristy appeared to me to be a sort of supernatural railroad terminal.

The ticket agent, dispatcher, and conductor, all in one, is the good lay-brother in charge. He keeps the traffic moving. First of all a strange priest coming in is greeted, cordially, with a smile. "Certainly you may say Mass; just wait a moment." An Army chaplain is removing his vestments. A Holy Cross Father introduces himself, two Monsignors, a priest from Denver, and one who, hearing mention of Syracuse, says he has been in Seneca Falls, a Franciscan preparing for a scheduled Mass. These are there. All strangers. But all utterly known for the priesthood within. All so at home, with almost identical gestures in picking up the amice, in placing the alb over the head, in crossing the stole, in the final lifting of a chalice.

The tracks in a railroad station are numbered; altars are not. They are named. So the lay-brother says: "You may use St. Joseph's altar . . . in the upper church." Or, "You had better

use the Holy Souls altar . . . in the lower church." The Blessed
Virgin's altar . . . the High Altar . . . St. Francis . . . the
Sacred Heart . . . the strangers are guided to them. Candles are
lit. The wine and the water are set out. "*Introibo ad altare Dei*
. . . I shall go unto the altar of God . . ." All through the morning. Strangers who know not each other's names, who never met
before, who may never meet again.

It does not matter to the people either, in the lower church
and in the upper church. They see a priest, in chasuble, vested,
approaching an altar. So . . . unless they are absorbed in Mass
at another altar . . . they make the sign of the cross with him,
and begin.

I had a server too. A young sailor who came out of the crowd.
He said afterward that he had a three-day pass from the New
London naval base, but that his home was in Wisconsin and
that he would have done better with the Latin if there had been
a card handy. He wanted to know if I knew a Father O'Brien in
Wisconsin, to which there could be but one answer. "Certainly."

HUMILES

O crest of all creation, pinnacle and height,
Past whom the Father's will chose not to soar
Nor tower more,
Thou arc of spread horizons and blue space,
Thou first, and through eternity,
Our last superlative,
Exemplar, plenitude, and mightiest,
O woman holding skies and tipping to the stars the light
That is their usefulness re-given for thy crown,
Hear thy renown!

We see thee in the molten gray of sea
Far brooding to the slant and margin cast
Of hooded sun,
And know thee there, the silvered Mary,
Stilled, contemplative.

The black storm thunders of thy three-day loss,
The tides are pressures of thy reaching prayer,
The gulls glide
On Magnificat, and in all calm
Thy quiet listenings live.

We find thee in the agonies of blood
That redden in the East and wound the West
To double death,
And know thee there, the severed Mary
Trust for deep redemptive.

And then we find thee glorious with gold,
Full drenched in gold above the open day
Of Summer's surf,
And know thee in the vesting, Mary,
God and Gabriel give.

But humblest of creation, lowliest and meek,
On whom the Father's merest wish may fall
To take thy all,
Thou total gift and whole obedience,
Surrendered self, in wanting brought
To willed diminutive,
Reversal, healing in thy scars our prides,
O woman of submission, faithful, turning to the Lord
Until thy heart is kneeling like the little hills,
Make so our wills.

. . . in the white

and walk of the morning:

The moon, dwindled and thinned to the fringe

of a fingernail held to the candle. . . .

MOMENT TO MOMENT

"Do you remember what you were doing on September 3, 1929? Probably not . . . unless you have an altogether exceptional memory." That is not the opening gambit in the District Attorney's case in a popular detective story, but rather the first two sentences in a book, reviewing the social history of the 1930's.

To think back on the 1930's is fascinating, for the events are near enough to be personal memories for most of us, and yet, so far removed across the chasm of World War II and the atomic bomb as to seem an ancient pantomime performed by a dimly remembered race. The NRA, the crash of the *Winnie Mae* with Will Rogers, the Big Apple, the Wickersham Commission, and the Kansas Sunflower, for example, are the names of distant shadows. If you are curious, the date of September 3, 1929, is mentioned in the history because that was the day when the Dow-Jones averages of stock-market prices made the high record of all time.

No man may say that this decade is without significance, but glancing swiftly through the whole narrative of our times, coming again on half-forgotten absorptions . . . Technocracy, Amos 'n Andy, the *Morro Castle* . . . it is difficult to escape the conviction that this is a newsreel and not too important, and that in a dozen years the very names here flashing will have lost all meaning. Mind you, we may grant the validity of interest in social change, of mass movement and trend, of statistics, and political problems, and especially in the hunger, the distress and the causes of war that hid in the '30's. We do need to be concerned, but I deny the real and personal importance of any history book of any decade written by anybody.

"Do you remember what you were doing on September 3, 1929? Probably not unless you have an altogether exceptional memory." Granted. We permit the historian to begin with his pivotal date. But even if you or I had that altogether exceptional memory, it does not follow that this date would be marked because the stock averages were at a record peak. Somebody must have been married on September 3, 1929, and that is what's important to him. The happy event will not be in the histories, but the significance remains. September 3rd may have been the date when little Willie had that operation. Maybe a new lawyer hung out his shingle then. Why, September 3, 1929, doubtless is somebody's birthday, and there is no argument against the real, the phenomenal importance of *that*. Or September 3rd may have been the evening of a gorgeous sunset. The air may have been filled with fragrance that night. Perhaps a hole-in-one enshrines this day, or a parting at a railroad station, or an entrance into the First Grade, or the achievement of a poem, or the beginning of a song, or a prejudice. To make an end of limitless human possibilities, this may have been the date when the cake didn't fall, and the cold-water frosting turned out right. The point here is that life is not lived largely, nor in multitudes, nor in trends of mass movement: it is lived singly, moment to moment, and no one can write the history of it except oneself.

But even by contrasting the small, the human, and the individual against the public, the social, and the general, we have not yet done with the argument that no one can point out the genuinely significant in any decade or on any date. Not by half have we exhausted the argument. Even that cake that was successful, even little Willie's operation are only temporarily important. We deal in much higher significance than the evanescent. September 3, 1929, may have been the date for a thousand Baptisms throughout the world, but if only it be the date for one Baptism, that, the Baptism, the beginning of God's grace in a soul, that is the importance of September 3rd, and by contrast, the Dow-Jones averages about the stocks are really silly numbers in a rather dull game.

September 3rd may have been the date when a soul strongly resolved to abandon evil. There may have been a sob of sorrow on that night. And that, you know is important. It is important forever.

How many Holy Communions were there on this morning? How many signs of the cross were made on how many brows? Did anybody on this date really see the meaning of a parable, or a beatitude, or a commandment? To come to the utter significance, what was the nature of the Judgment made for a single soul who has not known of the 1940's or the 1950's on earth?

Possibly there are no competent historians in existence other than the Guardian Angels, and by the same reasoning, there can be no proper and real estimate made of a decade unless all the Guardian Angels meet in a heavenly convention and compare notes. This notion, assuredly, is considered in all reverence and reality. Perhaps the Guardian Angels never sit around swapping mutual experiences. On the angelic level, history may be considered mere gossip. Angels know too much and they live in charity. That is why God made them, and why He made us. Real charity, if ever it universally conquered the earth, as it has won over the Angels, would mean the end of our history too, but it would mean the end of wars as it has meant the end of wars among the Angels. The proposition, therefore, that the Guardian Angels would assemble to discuss us is fantastic, and can only be derived from our darkened, earthy imagination.

But how might the story run . . . even the story of the '30's? That there was a happy day when an aviator named Corrigan flew to Ireland and said that he had flown the wrong way, while all the people laughed, for it was an innocent and holy joke, and he seemed like an ungoverned banshee. That there was a birth of five babies all in one birth in Canada, and apart from the consequent advertising and litigation, it was a significant and lovely event because children are beautiful, and the love of children is hopeful. The irresistible attraction of these five did many hearts good. It could be the Guardian Angels would say that. Or perhaps they would judge that a law was bad social legislation but that it was partially based on a human regard, and by that much was significant. Or that this Depression had cut down the divorce rate, but that hardly counts since expense is a low reason for not breaking, legally, a marriage. And we might be very sure of this: the seminaries, the cloisters, and the kitchens of home, the nurseries, the convents, the Societies for the Propagation of the Faith, the Chanceries, the Superintendents of School Offices, the backyard gardens, and the lawns with roller skates left on them at night, the far and lonely cabins of the missioners, the room of the scholar studying Aquinas under a lamp, these, all these . . . and permit me to include the parish rectory . . . maintained their usual importance through the 1930's, as they had in the '20's and the Teens, as they will through the '50's and on into the atomic era.

But honestly, I don't think the Angels would talk about us to each other. Only to God.

ECCLESIASTICUS

AFTER forty-two years of experience with himself, including six years of hard, realistic training in a seminary, and after almost seventeen years of some adventure and much daily routine in the priesthood, Father James K. Hyland, second assistant at St. Matthew's parish, Milton, was not easily convinced that he had seen a vision.

He was pacing now, back and forth, on the cement sidewalk that bisected the lawn between the rectory and the church. The air had the normal touch of chill to be expected at this season, the phlox beside the walk was mottled in purple, and between the puffs of his cigarette, he could anticipate the standings and the kneelings, and the final signs of the cross of the people within the church as they prepared to leave the pews of the Ten, spill out the doors, held open at last by the ushers to make room for the others beginning to come for the Eleven.

It was a simple, routine Sunday in Milton, and if he, Father Hyland, was the preacher, the assignment was only in line of duty, and he had met it hundreds of times before. Even the subject that fell to him in his turn was ordinary. He had stressed that announcement about the Bishops' Relief Collection, and then had talked in his sermon on the Eighth Commandment as indicated by the schedule of his Diocese for the Twenty-first Sunday after Pentecost. The thought that he was following orders, that he was doing what he was supposed to do, came to him as a momentary consolation. Why should he be upset? Why should he feel the faint touch of sweat on his forehead, and why, walking here, should he have to argue himself out of the notion that at the Ten O'clock Mass in Old Man Toomey's church, with Pete Gallagher about to pass the basket in the middle aisle and Tommy Alonzo nobly presiding at the side aisle, with the Junior Choir resting fitfully in the organ loft, with Jerry, the first assistant, sitting in the green vestments on the scamnum . . . he, Jim Hyland, standing in the pulpit and looking out over the congregation, had had a vision?

The thing was nonsense, of course. He took another drag on the cigarette and crushed it out under his heel. Better begin to get himself ready to preach again. The crowd was coming out the side entrance of the church already. The Eleven would be starting in ten minutes or less, and as he checked on his wrist watch, he smiled and nodded to the Myers family who said, "Good morning, Father," to him. Then he sought the quieter, less populous cinder schoolyard behind the church where the handball court and the base paths would be silent and deserted on this Sunday recess.

It was not that he didn't prepare his sermons. He was no St. Paul, Heaven knows, but neither was he so dull that they yawned at him, and certainly he was not a hypocrite. He at least made a try for sanctity, and running back in his mind, he could find no large flaw in the morning. He had risen in good time for the 7:45 Mass. Sunday thanksgivings were always hurried, yet he had knelt for a moment on the altar steps before going in to the rectory for orange juice and a cup of coffee. He had had a quick look at the football scores, had run up the stairs to the third floor, brushed the shoulders of his cassock after drying his face from the good cold water, had picked up his breviary, taken a swift glance again at the Sermon Outline, and had appeared, promptly and without fanfare, in the sacristy for the Nine O'clock.

And the Nine O'clock had gone fine. His voice had reached, he thought, most of the back pews under the loft, and that point about a lie against your neighbor had been like a stone dropped in a pond . . . the ripples, and the spreading disturbance . . . not bad, not bad at all. Why should he be worried? He didn't shout like the Old Man, and he never ascended the pulpit under the impression that he was Moses climbing Sinai. He couldn't quote the poetry as Dr. Francis Leverett was supposed to do over at Holy Trinity on the North Side, and he admitted that, except for a few phrases, he always thought it safer to read up on his Scripture citations. His memory was not as precise these later years, and he was beginning to find it easy to improvise on quick ideas that came in mid-paragraph. But he was no faker, he was no orator, and he had always judged that some human consolation could be granted to a man, even to a man who preached.

Why should any vision be loosed on him? Why should he be seeing things? Was he getting the scrups? What was that business at the Ten O'clock? He paused for a minute in his walking and stood watching the leaves in the oak tree in the yard, brilliant against the autumnal sky.

It was at the Ten O'clock that it had happened, without reason,

and without warning. He had read the Gospel, and then the congregation had settled down, and raised their faces to him. He
could see them, row on row, coalesced, amalgamated, reaching
back to the distant doors. A congregation. An assembly. His, for
a few minutes, to talk to. They were his wide and spread horizon.
Whole pewsful of them, massed and sitting close together in a
flock, and here, in the pulpit, he surveyed them in a view that
swept above them. He drew his breath and poised his voice . . .
a preacher.

Then it came, and although he was aware of no apocalypse,
though no sudden handwriting appeared on the church wall,
though he heard no sound as of a great wind and felt no fire
burning on his head, although it was a matter of seconds only, an
instant between the moment when he drew his breath and the
moment when he propelled it into his first word, Father James
Hyland had to argue with himself that he had not seen a vision.
The faces before him suddenly separated. They became a scene
made up of singulars. He found himself looking, not at a row
of heads, but at one head grown gray with worried years. Gulfs
came between persons and he saw, in an instant, not a congregation, not a massed and amalgamated group, but persons, isolated
and alone. He saw not plurally, but one, by one, by one.

Here in his pulpit, Father James Hyland saw what he had
always known: that a face is the one, unmultiplied Creation that
God had made to tell of the one, unmultiplied Creation which is
the human soul. That man there . . . the miracle of Tabor was
for him. That young girl in the feathered hat, and with the stroke
of adroit rouge . . . the parables were said to her. For that wife
wine had been made; for that boy, bread. Here was one who
needed love because his heart had drained; and over there, over
there near the pillar to the left, a face looked up as worn, as
urgent as a fisherman's face on the shores of Genesereth. There,
just there, before him in a pew was the woman at the well. Each
face became a world so subject to God's Providence and so need-

ful of God's hand, it was as though there were no other faces and no other worlds except this man and the unique, unduplicated world that is himself. Those two calm eyes, those two pools of expectancy before this pulpit were innocence and yielding to what he was about to say. And those two eyes, closed, resigned, waiting, searched for dreams to end the troubled dreams. For that child a command had been given permitting a close, intimate approach to the Divine. For that brow, white with convalescence, the powers of Heaven had been moved. For that ache, for that fear, for that love . . .

And if he, James Hyland, should be clumsy, should be hollow, if the right word did not fall from him: if he were dull, or merely literary, or if he were not literary enough: if he had the inept point: if his poised voice, sweeping out, should end with the awkward plea, the petty and banal paraphrase: if he were not blunt enough: if he were not kind . . . Those faces, one, by one, by one . . .

He had walked again around the corner of the church entrance and, entering the sacristy, had put on the lace surplice and the formal, tasselled stole taken from the drawer of the Solemn Set of vestments. Did he need a vacation, or was he just worried about himself? Was he slipping? Or could this really be, well, a sign of something, if not a vision?

He genuflected carefully before the carpeted steps of the high altar, and then knelt as the choir intoned the first verses of the "Come Holy Ghost." He remembered now that Toomey had rigorously insisted that, at the Eleven O'clock, the choir take time to chant the "Veni" for the Preacher. "Give the Last-Mass-Sermon dignity and a touch of the Cathedral," the Old Man had offered as a reason.

Father Hyland listened now to the ancient Latin words, and the ancient plea. Then he stood up, genuflected again, while his eyes focussed for a secret, heartening moment on the golden door of the Tabernacle. He turned, bowed liturgically to Jerry seated on the scamnum, walked briskly across the sanctuary, and set his foot on the steps leading up to the pulpit.

Later on that Sunday, the Evans family, talking about St. Matthew's as they passed the roast pork around the table and prepared the mashed potatoes with Mom's good gravy, heard the opinion of Uncle Stephen that Father Hyland didn't speak so well today at the Eleven, you could hardly hear him at times. And Cousin Louise added to the general interest of the Evans' Sunday dinner table by remarking that it must have been because he used up so much of his voice reading the Gospel. "I never heard Father Hyland so loud," she said. "He almost shouted himself hoarse when he was reading the Gospel."

MORE THAN NINE

THEY say that a cat has nine lives, but this is not true. A cat has only one life which is strictly limited to the experience of being a cat. That's the whole story; it is only a cat, and nothing more.

But with a man it is different. He really has nine lives, and perhaps others, if he happens to be an ambitious fellow. However, let's settle for the average, non-furious, calmer sort of person and say that his lives are merely nine. There is, first of all, the physical life, or the time spent in brushing his teeth, combing his hair, and getting down to his meals.

Then a man has his business life which may be anything from fixing dented fenders to selling insurance, to operating the American Air Lines, but which, in any case, comes under the general title of How to Get Cash.

Now I hate to use this next term because the headlines and the movies and the current fiction have ruined it, but, after his business life, there is his love life. That is his home, his wife, his children, those dear to him in heart, his friends, those close to him who are not as strangers. More often than not the How to Get Cash phase of living finds justification and sanction and value in what it contributes to his human loves, and the long labors and the worry and the fatigue in the marketplace are worth while because they are foundations of a home. The nine-to-five job, the night shift, the sales campaign, the estimate of costs and the margin of profit, the union dues are managed for the sake of the little circle of faces and the names that are his own.

It may be that business is also both the heart's desire and the mind's intent, and then there is the vocational life and he becomes a maker, a dreamer, a man absorbed in a career. Up to now we have only listed a few of everybody's lives.

There is the mental life, or that inner moving picture that keeps going even in sleep; the thoughts he thinks, the books he reads, the conversations he gets into; the recreational life or the games he bowls, the golf he shoots, the swims he swims, and the movies he sees; the political life, or how he votes and what he worries about in the international dispatches. There is the weather life consisting of straw hats or overshoes, satisfaction or discontent, too warm, too wet, too cold, and putting the chains on the car.

But there is yet one life that we have not mentioned, and it runs like a theme, like a bond and a tie and a continuity through all the lives, giving an ultimate significance and a final unity to everything. This is the one life that cannot be left out by anyone; it is the religious life, and it consists of meanings. This is what everything is about.

To think of one's religious life as a thread that weaves through the whole fabric is good for us because it may seem that religion is an affair only of moments. It is a moment of prayer, a Mass on Sunday, a quick petition to God when we are in need, a moment of acceptance to a grace, five minutes in the morning and five minutes at night, but always only a moment. Now religion is not that; it is not intermittent but continuous: it is not a segment but a whole; it is not a pool in isolation but a stream in movement.

Religion runs through and touches every least phase of human activity, and the way to get the most out of Catholicism, to really enjoy your Faith to the full is to realize the fact and consciously glory in it. It's great to be alive, but it's greater to be alive and know why.

Perhaps we ought to begin again at the basic physical life: look what religion does for that. In the first place sitting in that chair or pulling up to that dinner table is an action of the Temple of the Holy Ghost. This hair, that nose, ten fingers and ten toes are the House for the Indwelling of the Holy Spirit which is what the State of Grace means. Kneeling, genuflecting, being sprinkled with Holy Water, making the sign of the cross may bring the truth more obviously to mind, but it is always so, and, probably, we will be most conscious of it when these five senses of the physical life are one day anointed for their temporary end; but not for their end, because religion means that the mortal body *"puts on immortality"* and *"this corruption puts on incorruption."* Ever think of that? The flesh is to endure, you know.

Physical life is controlled by fast and by abstinence, is adorned by vesting, is ennobled by a feast, but let us get on to the matter of the business life where religion is much more pertinent than even adding machines and bank books. All business, buying and selling, hiring and firing, operates on a principle of justice, that is, the deep, undebatable notion that every man ought to be given that which is his due. You simply can't have any business unless you admit that principle. Debts ought to be paid, work done has the right to a reward, accounts ought to be honestly listed in a financial statement, a merchant ought to receive a profit for his pains. Everybody agrees to that; the marketplace could not run except for this general assumption. But why should all this be? Certainly this is justice, and any offense against it results either in a jail sentence, a loss of credit, or at least a bad reputation, but the point is, everybody agrees that such punishment is right and proper, and that nobody ought to be able to get away with cheating. Men concur in this even when they try to cheat. Why? Because justice is a virtue that looks outward from man to man, but it is based on God. Cheating is wrong . . . not merely foolish, or unprofitable, or impolite, but wrong in the nature of things, and all men know it. Justice is part of basic morality and is an expression of the way God made His earth.

When we come to what we have called the love life, we really discover the all-pervading and rich presence of the religious life. Except for religion, human love would either be a pretense or a tragedy. In God we know that this child, that mother, that father, this friend, all who may be dear, are not mere compositions of chemistry, are not mere developments of biology doomed to a quick and utter extinction. They are persons, and what we love in them is real and will not perish. Why is it that all the romances, all the songs, all the fairy tales even, speak of a "forever," and tell of "living happily ever after"? Because loss and defeat and separation would make human yearning a mockery if they were true. And the only "forever" is found in religion. What would the night be for a father who did not know this? What significance have the years, and graying hair, and the deep, creasing brow unless we are the children of God?

As for the mental life, did you ever imagine what it might be like if we could not have the thought of Christ? If nowhere on a man's yearnings there could be the healing touch of a prayer? As for the recreational life, how could there ever be laughter and gaiety and fun if there were only hiding and escape and trying to forget? The Communists have a silly phrase about religion being the opiate of the people. The fact is that the people would try to make everything an opiate except for religion. We can stand anything if hope survives. Religion runs through more of living than we realize, and we truly go on from day to day "through Him, by Him, and in Him."

There is even religion in our weather life. Is there not something Christmaslike in any snowflake, and is there not a secret and subtle suggestion of Easter in all the first murmurings of Spring?

GERARD MANLEY HOPKINS

AFTER these many years there is now in circulation a full American edition of the work of Gerard Manley Hopkins. Heretofore Father Hopkins has been available only in the slim rather special-looking volume edited by Robert Bridges, and containing only the major work, the poems which passed the exquisite and unrelenting standards set by the poet for himself. The new collection contains all the Hopkins that can be found, his unfinished work, his lesser efforts, his translations, and the simpler hymns which came out of his heart and did not have the full benefit of the anvil beat of his mind.

I would not claim that the new edition has made Hopkins easier to read, or that the prime necessity of reading him aloud has been avoided. He is still a subject for study, and after the study, for recitation. Furthermore each poem in his major work is still a thing in itself, an entity, almost a literature. He still disturbs the mind accustomed to the careless words and the uncounting phrases of lesser poetry. But now Hopkins is whole, as Shelley and Keats and Shakespeare are whole, with work that didn't quite come off, with half successes, and with the reassuring admission that there were scraps of paper left stuffed in his desk. The first quick consequence is that he looks human and as though he too had had to climb and struggle to gain the peak of Parnassus.

Gerard Hopkins was born in England in 1844. In 1866 he was received into the Catholic Faith by John Henry Newman. In 1868 he entered the Society of Jesus. He was ordained, worked as a parish priest, taught school, said his prayers, tried very, very hard to be a holy and fruitful man, wrote poetry in odd moments when his conscience let him do so, wrote letters and kept a journal, and then died toward the end of the nineteenth century. His work was not published until 1918, and it took ten years to sell out that first small edition.

But Father Hopkins was discovered by those who go looking for poetry and who could hardly be expected to know what the Faith-Jesuit-Sacerdotal-Conscience-Sacramental side of him was all about. He first appeared to be a sort of Picasso, if Picasso painted in the company and in the time of Rosa Bonheur, or like a Gershwin lost among the Stephen Fosters. It might even be said of him that he twinkled, a word which, I confess, has a special and odious meaning for me in regard to anybody's poetry. A cult of Hopkins arose with some pretty heavy brains included in the eclectic circle. But Father Hopkins has survived. He could not quite be hidden behind his interpreters. He is bursting out into the hardier weathers of the language, and the new, fuller edition will, let us pray, help him out to the steady ocean and away from the narrows.

One of the critics has said that Catholics are prone to grab at Father Hopkins and exhibit him as "our man" in poetry because he was a convert and had the good sense to join the Jesuits, but that his value is that of an artist and not that of an apologist, however rare such be in unique poetry. I do not join the issue, nor indeed consent to that real temptation, but I will argue to the hilt of strength that the full appreciation of Father Hopkins awaits that moment when he is discovered to be a poet of the soul, the conscience, and the everlastingly difficult vocation of trying for holiness on the inside. His best poems are spiritual, and can be best understood by the Catholic mind. They can be like a native speech to the cloisters. They are best read in the period of one's own examen of conscience or shortly afterward. The chief and central drive in Father Hopkins is identical with that found in St. Augustine, St. Teresa of Avila, and in the soul of any man on earth who tries to match, however far off, the full Fiat of Our Lady. Unless this spiritual urge and force and experience is seen to be the premise of the poetry of Gerard Manley Hopkins, his effect is only partially felt, and his meaning is largely lost.

For instance, "Felix Randal" is the finest major poem in the language on the meaning of Extreme Unction and the Priesthood that administers the Sacrament. Again, "The Bugler's First Communion" is human in its pity, but keeps eager sight of the Divine Gift of Christ. The theme of struggle, of spiritual effort, of darkness and light, of wonder at God, of spiritual perseverance runs through almost all of the Hopkins work like the central message of a great retreat. This, of course, is nothing new to anyone who has ever really read Hopkins, but it seems to need emphasis and repetition. One of the most lyric praises of the Mother of God in English is here. And in the series of sonnets called by the scholars "the terrible sonnets," there is suffering, anguish, resolution and resignation enough for a saint. Maybe it was.

Among the new and minor verses now available is one, "Jesu Dulcis Memoria." In the Hopkins work this is very simple. It is, indeed, childlike with the traditions of the Faith as they ought to be. I suggest that it be read with Holy Communion in mind, or as a thanksgiving prayer, as a meditation for some holy morning that has been blessed with the reception of the Sacrament. "Jesus to cast one thought upon makes gladness after He is gone, but more than honey and honeycomb is to come near and take Him home. Song never was so sweet in ear, word never was such news to hear, thought half so sweet there is not one as Jesus, God the Father's Son. . . . Jesu, a springing well Thou art, daylight to head and treat to heart, and matched with Thee there's nothing glad that can be wished or can be had. Wish us good morning when we wake and light us, Lord, with Thy day-break. Beat from our brains the thicky night and fill the world up with delight."

The notion once occurred that someone might put these lines to simple and easy music, but now I think not. They ought to be read quietly, and on one's knees.

TAKE YOUR TIME

THE page was turned and then, as happens too infrequently in casual reading, came a sentence to halt the mind: "Years are short, only the days are long." A melancholy sort of observation, but true enough. Days are long because we are in the midst of living them. Years are not long since they only exist either in memory or in anticipation, and who is there that will look at the improbable figure of his age and really believe it? A man may admit his age. He may accept it. He may even boast of it, or more likely, joke about it. But he rarely believes it. Age is true for other people, observable, subject to comment, not to say speculation, but age is never personal. Simply it does not happen to us.

Once you start thinking on such a theme there is no end. A phrase in one book recalls others. All the poetry, all the epigrams, the philosophy, the moralizing, the counsels, the consolations, the prescriptions that have to do with time! "Barefoot boy with cheek of tan." "Backward, turn backward, O time in thy flight." "Time heals all things." And the Emperor who said to the troops ranked beside the pyramids, "Twenty centuries look down on you." The direful inscription said to have been on the sun dial: "It is later than you think." The programs that note: "Time: The Present." And then, true to life: "Act III: Years Later." And even radio which sells, mind you, sells time.

Some day an enterprising and ambitious scholar will compile a book filled with such references. The volume would be a hefty one and it would belong to no culture nor to any single rank of mentality. Time and its awareness, its run and leap, its poignancy, problems, and decisions are the common experience of the race. If the book were really exhaustive, it would have sections like an encyclopedia. Imagine the whole department that would be taken up merely with songs. "When It's Apple Blossom Time

Etc." "Springtime in the Etc." "That Old Gang of Etc." "Memory
Etc." Amazing when you begin to go into it.

Banks pay interest for time. Insurance companies compute
and make book on it, if such language is permitted. The most
mystic and marvelous statements in our speech use time as a
verb. "Two times two are four." No past or future about that,
and there is no other way to state it. Two times two are four,
and we mean times and we mean are, and let the sceptics, sub-
jectivists, and those who don't believe in God fuss around with
that.

That's the only way to take time, the way the Faith takes
it. Outside the Faith days and years and age are problems. We
are told to enjoy time for it is fleeting, kill it for it is a bore,
endure it for it is a burden, forget it for it is a sorrow, hope for
it because it is a future, or yearn for it because it is a past. Only
the Faith says: "Coin it for it is a present." The Faith can afford
to look time in the face because the Faith is arched to the eterni-
ties, the one before time began and the new one which will begin
when time ends. The Faith is not afraid of time and uses it as a
grace. Matins, Lauds, Prime, Vespers . . . Matins, Lauds . . .
this is time made holy, a veritable sub-sacrament. The Faith can
make time to be the element, the channel for Divine Grace. Advent, Christmas, Lent, Pentecost, doubles, semi-doubles, vigils, fast
days, death days for martyrs which are called birthdays, and the
process of running into time which is called a Retreat. That's the
very schedule of the Faith, and it is noted and directed by a little
manual, like a calendar, which is called, mark you, an Ordo. Exactly, an Ordo because the Faith orders time, makes sense out
of it, gives time a reason for being time which is a difficult achievement, and one quite impossible except in the Faith.

Michael Angelo once made a famous and beautiful statue of
Our Lady as she received the Crucified from the Cross. Critics
told him that he had made a bad error because he had carved the
Mother with a countenance younger than her Son's. The artist is

supposed to have replied that he intended it that way because Mary, in her sweetness and in her grace, was aloof from the scars of sorrow and pain. It is a beautiful thought and yet most unsatisfactory. Our Lady was not aloof. That's the whole strength and appeal and urge of her. She was real. But if she is to be portrayed as youthful and very dear, may we not better think that the cause is her absorption, full of grace, in eternity, that her eyes never wavered from seeing the everlasting things? That she looked not away, nor was distracted? That she made no errors in value, and in that she is very young? It is the morning star . . . the dayspring. . . .

BEADWORK

It does not take very much experience with life to discover that all seasons happen suddenly except Summer. We wait so long for Summer, we look forward to it so ardently, in late May and June we wonder so wistfully if this dubious and indecisive warmth is the genuine season, we search so eagerly for signs that we can hardly say that Summer sneaks up on us. It is not so with any other time of the year; all other seasons are surprises. You may still be in the Fourth of July mood when you notice that shops are advising the purchase of Christmas cards. Mentally you may be lagging still around Thanksgiving when the priest announces the fast days for Lent. One day you look out the window and almost it seems by some sudden conspiracy, the rain is half snow; brown leaves are all over the driveway; you pause to put on the half-forgotten coat before going out. October has happened while you turned your head.

All that, of course, is common experience. But with a priest the seasons hide an extra, a sort of vocational surprise, and it is this: a page in the Ordo is turned and suddenly the Month of the Rosary is here. The Ordo, we hasten to explain, is just what the name implies, an ecclesiastical calendar, a time-table for the soul, a schedule for the spiritual, a route map for the prayers. It is printed in Latin and is so ingeniously abbreviated that railroad tables, stock-market reports, and those mysteries they print on sports pages about horses, seem, by comparison, to be expansive and copious abundance. And the Ordo, like the seasons it records, is a constant surprise.

For example, page 362 is flipped over and here's what hits you on 363: "I Rosar Mense Octbri Jussum. S. R. C. Ur et Or 26 Aug 1886 decrevit in omnib Cathol Orbis." No, it's not nonsense or esoteric gibberish. It means October has come, but since we live in the Faith, it means that October has been ordered by the Sacred Congregation of Rites, in a decree dated August 1886, to be, for the City and the World, the month of the Rosary. History, tradition, the exercise of high authority within the Church, devotion, the formal consecration of time, the love of Our Lady, and the familiarity of the little string of beads are all here, set down in Latin abbreviation in the pages of a schedule used from Maine to Manila and from Florida to Singapore. October in the Faith means beads in the hand and a strong, sweet season in the soul.

You will, surely, be interested in a further quotation from the Ordo? "II Indiae Rosarii (Coll 1937 .. 360)." Are you not interested? You ought to be for this is the Ordo presenting the list of Indulgences and the conditions for gaining them through the Rosary. An Indulgence, you know, is an act of jurisdiction performed by the Church, as the Church has been empowered by Christ, that lets you out of some of the punishment you deserve for your sins. It's worth getting, that release from the punishment, as anyone with sense knows. You see, when a genuine, complete, real, mortal sin is committed it deserves, and might get, Hell. Nobody can push you past that danger except yourself. You have to be really sorry for the sin, honestly pledge not to do it again, and seek then the forgiveness of Christ through the Sacrament, Penance, He most mercifully gave for that purpose.

That's the only way out of the danger of Hell. You have to escape by yourself.

But supposing you are all set. You are sorry, you have reformed, and you have been absolved after a good confession. Is the score back to zero again? Is it all over? It is not.

The sin is actually forgiven, the risk of Hell, for this sin, at least, is done with, but you still owe something. Indeed you do. There is punishment even though the sin is gone and Hell no longer threatens, and you must either punish yourself now by your own choice, or wait for God to do it later in Purgatory. However it is done, this limited and smaller penalty must be paid. It is just and it must be met. That is why we don't eat meat on Friday, and observe all those fast days and give up amusements once in a while, and discipline ourselves generally. These are free punishments and are meant to balance the account. And besides there are little sins, too small to deserve Hell, and these must be paid for too. You can't just skip anything, you know. Facts are facts even when they are only little sins like being nosey and mean and sarcastic.

Now in this situation, the great, watchful, kindly Church stands empowered with the merits of Christ, with the merits of Our Lady, and with the merits of the saints and holy people who fasted more than they had to, who said so many more prayers than they needed themselves, and who never committed much sin at all. And when you do some good work, like visiting a church, like making the sign of the cross devoutly, the Church gives to you, just for the good work, what somebody else earned for you. You are let off from some of that punishment you will have to meet. That's what an Indulgence is. And during October, the month of the Rosary, the rich Indulgences are given for saying your beads.

We ought to note well that you can't qualify for an Indulgence while in a condition of mortal sin. As long as there is the risk of Hell, there is no use even thinking about these lesser punishments, and the way out of them. You have to get yourself past the danger of Hell before you are even ready to work on the minor penalty. Indulgences are only for people who have been rid of major sin and are eligible to pay off what comes after.

But opportunities await us all in October and through the easy and happy saying of Our Lady's beads! The Ordo again lists them for us. If you recite, with pious mind, the five decades of the beads before the Blessed Sacrament . . . that is, inside your parish church . . . you get a full remission of all you owe for all your sins, as often, as many times, as you recite the five decades there, even though you don't recite them all at once, but still in the same day. Isn't that something? The Church calls this Indulgence a Plenary one because it is complete. You have to go to Confession and Holy Communion, either a little while before you recite the beads or a little while after. That is necessary also for the Indulgence. If you say the beads on a Monday or Tuesday, you need to go to Confession and Communion the next week end or the week end previously. But it is all so generous, and if you have the proper disposition of soul, you may gain the full cancellation of your account.

In addition, and because this is the Month of the Rosary, you can gain the same full Indulgence by saying the beads, even outside a church and far from the Presence of the Blessed Sacrament, on the Feast of the Rosary, October 7th, and any and all of the whole eight days following. October is a month of opportunity.

Some of the Indulgences, let us observe, go with the physical use of the beads so, to gain everything, the Church expects you to hold the beads in your hand and pass them through your fingers, to meditate in your mind on the Mysteries of the Birth, the Suffering, and the Resurrection of Our Lord as best you can. There is no need for a great, elaborate fuss. Just think for a few seconds on those Mysteries before a new decade is begun. And don't forget the prayer you must say for the intention of the Holy Father.

It's a good idea to say the Holy Father's prayers . . . a few Our Fathers and Hail Mary's and Glorias . . . every day so that you can be sure.

RELAX!

WITHIN the great household of the Faith there are all kinds and varieties of Catholics. Our Lord knew that and intended the Church to be such an institution for He compared the Church to a net cast into the sea and, on occasion, to a tree of which He said: *"all the birds of air dwell in the branches thereof."*

We are not all the same, indeed we rather resent the assumption that all Catholics are alike. There are ardent Catholics and luke-warm Catholics (poor people), Sunday Catholics and everyday Catholics, Irish, Italian, and Dutch, people who use the envelope system, and those who don't. There are those who think the pastor is a fine fellow and those who sympathize with the parish-ioners, Catholics who are devoted to the Little Flower and those who prefer saying their prayers through St. Francis. There are generous Catholics and niggardly Catholics, First Friday ones, Holy Name and non-Holy Names. There are parochial-school Catholics and those whose children are deprived, bemedaled Catholics and scapulared Catholics. There are those who read and those who rely on best seller lists, Lenten Catholics and those who won't enjoy Easter . . . the blind, the lame, the halt, the sinners and the saints, the belligerent and the peaceful. We are a varied people.

But every Catholic in the world, no matter what the state of his soul, does expect certain things of the Church and is content and at ease in mind when the Church acts as he expects the Church to act. Anything contrary would shock and horrify him. No matter what his personal response, his whole scheme of things, the whole pattern of his thought would be blasted to bits if the Church didn't do what he knows the Church will do. Thus every

Catholic, even a fallen-away Catholic, expects the Church to be in favor of marriage and against divorce. Anything else is unthinkable. He expects the Church to be concerned with education, to be zealous for the Commandments, to be urgent in the matter of the Sunday worship, to be scrupulous and divinely serious over the Sacraments, and really to act on all occasions as though religion were the most important thing in the world, which it is.

Every Catholic expects the Church to have the charity which is the Heart of Christ. That we are very sure of. That is fundamental. We expect the Church to teach love of neighbor, to care for the orphan and for the poor, to minister to the sick, and to be watchful over the suffering everywhere. Our whole world would be put in reverse if this were not true. We should be shocked and stricken, grieved, and shamed, and horrified, and we couldn't sleep nights if the Church, the Church of Christ, the Church of our love and of our childhood, if the Church did not keep charity as the first and most binding of the virtues.

The thing is impossible (O, thank God!) but let us for a moment suppose that all the sermons of a Sunday went like this: "My dear friends, we have the poor all about us, there is human suffering in the world, but don't bother your heads. Don't fuss. Suffering is no concern of yours. Are you your brother's keeper? Let 'em starve! Squeeze every nickel you can get your hands on for thou shalt love thyself and let thy neighbor take care of himself. Be smart. We have enough to do to manage for ourselves. Amen."

Can't you imagine how you would feel if you heard that some Sunday? It's a nightmare, isn't it? Your whole world would crumble, and would there not then be fear, real fear, in your soul? Of course. Then you would be seeing not failure in yourself which you can understand, but you would be seeing failure in the Church which you could not for a moment endure!

But don't worry. The Church will be true to Christ; the Church will be true to you. The Church doesn't fail you; the Church will always act as you expect and want and intend the Church to act. You can still go on being proud of the Church even though you are one of those Catholics who never helps very much. The Church is still the Church, so relax.

"FOR HIS PART"

IT IS very nearly impossible, once inside, to mistake a Catholic church. A certain, forthright supernaturalness is all about. The place is fairly filled with a normal, plain, uninhibited sense of the other world, as if this building were set here to be a visible framework for contact with a higher and a surrounding series of invisibles. A feeling of communication, of giving and receiving, is very strong.

People kneel before statues and look up to them, and you are aware that beyond the statue, which is only plaster, outside, somewhere in God's place of souls, a conversation, a petition is being made with a person. The Stations really do call up the ancient Drama of the Darkened Day, and bring it here. The red vigil lights are really watching. All the altars bear an air of waiting for morning. The extraordinary, the crashing sentences, the hopes and the demands of the Gospels, the thundering speech of Christ, the huge issues and visions, the troops of angels caught in His words, the reversed values in the parable stories, are all held here, hanging in the silence like premises, but like something normal and assumed and routine.

A Catholic church is alive with the supernatural. And the sanctuary lamp, the one direction pointed in all the genuflections, the focus for eyes, for prayers, for flowers, for architectural lines, on the Golden Door give witness to the Presence of Him Who is there in Body and in Person, dwelling, inhabiting, and Who is known to be so.

As the total atmosphere of any Catholic church is unmistakable, so also is the special identification of the churches of various nationalities. You would never confuse an Italian church with an Irish church. Some vividness of the appointments, some generosity in candles or lights or decoration, some choice in the saints represented in the statues, the use of glass to frame them, would instantly declare the Latin.

A French church would have its own inward slant, its own angle, like a slab for the wood of the altar. The lace and the woven gilt edges would be distinctive.

Some touch of Bavaria, a wood carving, a special love of cribs and Christmas would mark the German. Over all, indeed, are the warmth and life of the positive supernaturalness of the Catholic, but shaded and made subtly different by history and ancestry.

And the building of which we would tell now had that implication of vigor, the coloring, the humanity, the sight of a saint in armour and with a sword and a globe, which indicates the Slavic.

Perhaps the incident is much too slight to have significance, but in the Faith even a casual gesture can be important, and in this simple and brief scene both that sense of Catholic reality before the supernatural and the special sense of family branches within the Faith are involved.

It was late afternoon during the time of the Forty Hours. The door of the front vestibule opened and two nuns came in. You could hear their footsteps first, then the noise of the door, and then they were moving down the aisle with that swift, silent, ordered, but free and confident progress which nuns exhibit when they come into a church intent upon a definite task.

They opened and went through the altar gate, first one, then the other, black-veiled, quiet. They knelt, and in a profound double genuflection, they bowed before the Blessed Sacrament. They bent so utterly low that you could not see them from the church side of the sanctuary rail. They had disappeared completely. It was a measurable second or so that they were gone. Then, upright again, they remained a moment or so in prayer before rising, the one to go to the sacristy, the other to lift a candelabra from the altar to carry it after her Sister.

This was routine practice of the Faith. Nothing special. But it must have been that bow, so low and reverent, with the nuns disappearing behind the marble rail that made it impressive. Here was direct, joyous knowledge that Our Lord was on the altar. They knew, just like that, that He was there. They loved Him and greeted Him in a profound salute, spoke to Him a while after they had walked into His Presence, and then they went to serve Him, to care for His place of Presence.

There is no need to get into the exactness of theological accuracy for the moment, nor to be concerned with precise theological expression, but as Our Lord looked out from behind the white appearance of the Host, as He saw that careful and most horizontal bow, as He took this reverence and observed there the real and alive and genuine knowledge that He was Real, as He took this love and devotion, do you not think He was glad within Himself?

He was already giving them happiness. He had granted them much of the "*hundred-fold.*" But He knew that for His part, in exchange, as it were, for this deep bow, He was keeping so much more. He was holding so much more than these Sisters could know of or estimate. His secret in His Own Heart for the hereafter, for the time when the supernatural above and in eternity, beyond this church, should be passed, was so much more than they now had. It must be pleasing to Him, His secret, His Own knowledge of what He was saving for them. And He would smile to Himself within the Host for the greatness of the surprise these two would one day discover?

And if Our Lord looked out from His place above the disappearing Sisters, He would have seen in the back of the church in one of the pews, a father with four sons. The sons were a year apart in age and the oldest could not have been more than nine. They had come in and were saying their prayers, and the youngest had to be made to sit quietly and be still. They were learning of Our Lord to Whom the Sisters bowed. They were learning of Him from their father at this Forty Hours, for he had brought them here, and had come himself to point Our Lord out to them. Later he sent three of them down to light some vigil lights, and they were all fascinated with the business of the tapers and the matches, and the choice of which candles to light. The youngest was kept in his seat, but he shared in the triumphant return of the three.

As I say, when He looked out and observed the children in addition to the Sisters, was He not happy for them, too, because He had so much, over and above, to give them also? Theirs was a Catholic home, with parents and bonds that cannot be severed, a home where holy pictures are, and a knowledge that the Forty Hours were in progress and that the children should be brought. They already had so much happiness in Him, He had already given them the very best in living, and did He not smile again to think of what else awaited this father and his four sons?

A fidelity to Him is always voluntary, either in individuals or in nations, it is always freely given and retained because it is willed not to be lost. The practice of the Faith is exactly this: a gift made to Christ. It can be withheld. It can be refused. But if it be given, then Our Lord is Himself free to return what He freely would give, and it is so much more than any of us know.

He must be pleased Himself to think of that? He must look out for the little gestures and be glad for them? He must enjoy the various ways and mannerisms of the Faith? But there is no question: He is happy for the bowing of the Sisters, and glad that the father and four sons were here, and He thought, no doubt, of their mother cooking supper at home and who would be down for devotions in the evening.

MINOR SIGNS

IN ADDITION to the major evidence for the divine foundation of the Church, there are innumerable minor signs that constantly indicate that the Church has been fashioned by the hand of God. By the major evidence, of course, we mean that the Church is One in the midst of a divided humanity, that it is Holy in the midst of indifference and evil, that is Universal among segments and division, that it is Apostolic in the midst of the disinherited. To sum up, the Church is like nothing else in the world and stands before human observation, singular, unparalleled and alone.

But over and above this great central proof, we can discover a whole series of smaller, slighter indications which serve to confirm the established conclusion.

For example, the teaching of the Church in regard to marriage and divorce is much more than a consistent attitude that refuses to bend before mere fashion. What the Church has to say about a husband and wife is what the inner heart of a man would expect the Church to say if the Church were founded by God. The doctrine conforms to his best instincts. This is what he knows in his dreams to be true: this is what his highest poetry and his best songs are all about: this carries the persuasion of truth: this is worthy of the Divine.

Or again, the Church seems to have been inspired to a knowledge of things which the psychologists are only just now finding out. The Faith used windows and lights and color to tell of God long before such approaches were used to sell cigarettes. The Faith had things you could hold on to in your prayers, beads, medals, scapulars, holy water, palms and ashes, long before such methods were judged useful in classrooms, in hospitals, in asylums and in kindergartens. Somehow the Church seems to have had advance information about human nature and how to guide it.

That, we may claim, and in all reverence, is another straw to show the Wind that blows through this structure.

And lastly, the Church never said to any man that his salvation was assured. No soul has ever, as long as life lasts, been looked upon as "saved." There is always the need for a quiet time that a man may consider where he stands. There is always a reconversion job to be done. Human nature requires it, a divine wisdom counsels it, and that is why for all of her own, for the priests, for the Bishops and the monks and the Cardinals, for the Pope himself, for all Sisters and Brothers, for everybody, an annual period of retreat is prescribed. By strict Canon Law religious people are obliged to forget all work, all plans, all labor, even though it be for the Church, and to go apart, alone, to examine the conscience, to renew the motivation in Christ, to correct faults, and to make fresh resolution.

So the annual retreat is a sign: it is a sign that a more than human prudence is at work here. The world may judge, perhaps rightly, that the good Sister is an obvious saint: the Church says, "Make your retreat just the same, my dear."

THE NAMES

DURING the month of November the altar in nearly every parish church has, resting on it somewhere, a neat pile of black-bordered pages listing the names of hundreds of the dead. The pages are compiled previous to All Souls Day, and are intended to identify a specific share in the Three Masses of the Day, and to be a constant memento during this whole season when we remember the deceased.

I have often thought that these familiar lists are among the most eloquent documents of Catholicism. They are eloquent of the Faith certainly, for they are a practical exercise in the human doctrine, the Communion of the Saints. They say that the Faith does not let go at death but rather endures. They declare that the

dead are not gone from us but are joined to us in the bond of
Christ. They name the dead but mean life; they are a list useful
nowhere except on a Catholic altar.

The world has cancelled these names. They no longer appear in
directories, in telephone books, in tax rolls; these are names that
concern no business, no society; they are not part of current
problems and worries. But the Faith has not cancelled them: they
do appear in this listing. They are the concern of the Church, and
every last one of them is part of the eternal watching of the
All Souls prayer.

And yet, beyond this primary and mortal significance, the
lists are also eloquent for what they reveal of the living, for what
they disclose about the Catholics who write them and hand them
in each year. The Holy Day looks both ways, and it might be
interesting to pause a moment over what the November custom
indicates of Souls who do the giving and not the receiving.

I do hope this will not seem too bold a mediation, nor an in-
trusion in a private, personal affair. True, Catholics generally do
not review the All Souls intentions as written down. The pages
rest on the altar. But there is no secret about them; they are not
under a seal; and if I presume to mention what the lists contain,
you will discover, I am sure, only what you already knew though
you have never opened the envelopes and placed these human,
prayerful pages one on top of another on the eve of All Souls.

To begin, the great majority of the lists conclude with the
words: "And for all the souls in Purgatory." That is, very nearly,
a unanimous last entry. There is a catalogue of relatives and
friends and intimates, and then, almost in a rush, in a sort of
spiritual hurry, the inclusive, final embrace . . . "for all the
souls." It is as though a Catholic family, grateful for the strength
of the Faith, happy in the thought that their own are to be remembered, are eager not to seem selfish, and intend to take in
everybody. They want the beloved remembered, but they wish
no one to be forgotten. It is a kind of scrupulosity in charity. It

is a universal, final gesture. Perhaps we have here a reflex of Catholic training, for all Catholic prayers for the dead end that way; we may even find here the compulsion of the Catholic spirit; certainly we have in this devoted postscript something of great eloquence.

The lists reveal, too, the family character of religious life. You can see the old, old truth here. You find on these pages evidence of what the Catholic home is, and the mystic, profound and holy linking which is Catholic marriage. You can trace it all in the way the names fall out. First there are the names of the husband's relatives, the paternal grandparents and kin, and then there are the names of the wife's relatives, and the maternal grandparents and kin, and lastly, there may be names of the children born of the marriage and gone on to God ahead. It is like a genealogy for eternity, a family tree for Heaven.

Most of the lists are taken up with relatives, possibly because the page is short and possibly because people presume that friends will be included in their own family lists. To be sure, a recent death in a parish, a death even in recent years, will be traced all across many lists like a repeating prayer. There is eloquence in that also. But as a steady rule these pages for All Souls follow the families, like faces in the Sunday pews, like children and names coming up in a parish school.

Some lists give the full, formal names in detail. Others, in a kind of ancient, Christian simplicity simply declare: "Mother, Grandfather, Daughter, Sister, Aunt." It makes no difference, of course, since God in His goodness needs no labels nor the correct spelling of a name. Either method is valid and useful, but I detect in the simple naming of the living bond, in the single word, "Father," or "Daughter," the old instincts of the Faith. It is even more striking in the lists that say: "For James, and John, and Ellen, and Mary." That's the way the Requiem runs for pontiff or prince, for saint or for sinner. The baptismal name is sufficient identity.

Lastly, let me mention one of the most eloquent points of all in the November remembering. It is surprising how many lists contain hidden or anonymous gifts. There is the page that says: "For the most forgotten soul." There is the page that says: "For the soul that is nearest to Heaven," and "For the soul that has nobody on earth." These are lovely spurts of the Christian charity. They are like little human expressions of pure goodness. They are like friendly waves across the years. One page will declare: "For the souls that loved Our Lady," and another will say: "For the soul that suffers for faults most like mine," and another, "For the soul that offended as I offend."

And the sacrifice of the war is not forgotten. The lists are filled with G. I.'s each year, and the dead that fell from Iwo to the Bulge.

The priests? The Sisters? Those who worked and themselves prayed for souls? What would you think? Of course. Of course the priests and the Sisters are here on the lists. These are pages written by a Catholic people. They reflect the minds of a Catholic people. Of course the sanctuaries and the convents are here. These names, written by folk who are concerned with their own, are the most eloquent of all.

HARVEST

IT IS obvious to anyone, even to one who does no more than look out of a window, that another year on earth is ending. The long cycle of the months is coming to a conclusion. The golden fabric of the autumn leaves is tattered and already there are holes in it where trees are black and bare. The fields are brittle stalks; the hills are brooding, and they have subsided to a still and passive waiting beneath the rains. The harvests are all in. Work is done. The opulent promises of summer are all fulfilled. Another year on earth is ending.

Now all this to a Catholic is deepened and enriched and made to be more than a season by the divine transformation of the Faith. What is merely a natural experience is lifted, in the Faith, to a supernatural meaning, for the Faith places All Saints Day and All Souls Day against the background of the denuded trees, the harvested fields, and the earth that has yielded all that it has to yield.

These November Feast days are the holy days of humanity. They are harvest days. They are days that tell the ultimate consequence of all the labor and the promises of life. They are, in a sense, the ending of the story. They are summary and completion for the souls of men, and they tell the garnering of what Bethlehem and Calvary and Pentecost planted.

On All Saints Day and on the following Day of All Souls, the vision of the Church sweeps backward through the ages since Christ and sees all the generations that have come and are gone. There are whole nations and empires in that view. There are names and families and dynasties and tribes and races and genealogies. The Church sees the ruins of cities and the silent places in the dust.

She surveys houses and homes that are no longer warm with a hearth, thrones that are empty, roads that are breached by weeds, marketplaces where bargaining no longer cries. She sees hands that have dropped the books, arms that have left the plow, gowns and cassocks and habits and cowls that are no longer worn; estates left uncontested, medals that are lost to meaning, and the faces, the dense, nameless multitudes of faces: and the Church ponders, then, the harvesting of Christ. The story is done and the end has come. And so the vision of the Church cannot remain within the horizons of earth nor within the limits of time. There is nothing to see except the remnants of lives that are gone, and leaving the earth, the Church keeps All Saints Day for the vanished souls who are in the Presence of God, and All Souls Day for the vanished lives that are waiting for the Presence of God.

These are the ultimate human Feasts. They are the November of our humankind. They are the days of harvest.

There are few minds which do not sense the power of these autumn holy days. Both days are vast and both are personal; they are enormously satisfying. Paganism never had anything remotely comparable. Science must look only at the ruins and the remnants. Sentiment has been able to reach only a tear and a mood of poignant sadness. The states, the cities, the empires only lay a wreath and build cold stone to a monument. The Faith has left the earth, and, in Christ, through Him, by Him, and in His power, the Faith keeps All Saints Day and All Souls Day. It is the end of the story; there is no more.

When you think of it, these holy days of the dead are the last feast days of the year. After them Advent begins and the Faith commences another year in its earthly history. There is no more for the Church to do now, but to start all over again, and that is why, after All Saints and All Souls, we come to the Feast of December 8th, the Immaculate Conception of Our Lady.

This is the preparation for Christmas. This is the day that tells of the Adornment given by God to the soul of Mary in the last yearning glory of the Old Testament. The love of God for men begins again in the grace that shielded her from sin and began the destruction of evil. Mary is the spring before the Spring. She is the dawn that came before the Light. She is the pre-beginning and is both anticipation and accomplishment. Her Immaculate Conception is the pre-echo of the Word. When the year ends in the spiritual November, the Church begins again with a vision of her virginal Spring.

Then Advent will be complete and the bells of midnight will ring for the Nativity. A Child will be born Who is Life for all generations, and we shall see the shepherds coming, the first of All Saints, and the Wise Men approaching, the first of All Souls. Another cycle will begin, as it must begin, for there is nothing left after the harvest, except another harvest in another year.

Nihil Obstat:

VERY REV. VINCENT M. MAYER, O. F. M., CONV.
        Censor Librorum

Syracuse, N. Y.
June 9, 1951

Imprimatur:

✠ WALTER A. FOERY
        Bishop of Syracuse

June 11, 1951